T0193989

Conversations
with
Augusta

ALICE MARIE THORP DUXBURY

CONVERSATIONS WITH AUGUSTA

iUniverse books may be ordered through booksellers or by contacting:

iUniverse
1663 Liberty Drive
Bloomington, IN 47403
www.iuniverse.com
1-800-Authors (1-800-288-4677)

ISBN: 978-1-4917-7244-7 (sc)
ISBN: 978-1-4917-7246-1 (hc)
ISBN: 978-1-4917-7245-4 (e)

Library of Congress Control Number: 2015911264

Print information available on the last page.

iUniverse rev. date: 09/09/2015

To Gerald Max Thorp
1927–1983

Table of Contents

Acknowledgments

Dr. Marion Clark (deceased), Marguerite's close friend, who sent me a treasure of personal photos, articles, and documents concerning Marguerite's life and career shortly after Marguerite's death in 1972.

My sons, Mark Thorp Duxbury and Gilbert Shawn Duxbury, both of whom provided encouragement and found subtle humor in family history. A special thanks to Mark for allowing me the use of his computer, for restoring family photographs, and for providing essential technological assistance.

My nieces, Gerald's daughters, Terry Fortner and Suzanne Thorp, for their contributions to the family history, and for Suzy's memory of Augusta's fondness for lily-of-the-valley cologne. Both have devoted valuable time and effort in the creation of *Conversations with Augusta*.

Gail Grieb, archives specialist at DuPont-Ball Library, Stetson University, Deland, Florida, who provided copies of correspondence and other documents relating to Marguerite's years at Stetson and subsequent position at Virginia Intermont College, Bristol, Virginia.

My second cousin, Della Shafer, for locating and sending online information about Oscar, providing genealogical charts and information about the Thorp family, and allowing me to include an account of a family tragedy and a photo of G. W. Thorp with one of his inventions.

Anne Shumaker, PhD, Virginia Intermont College, Bristol, Virginia, who provided copies of documents relating to Marguerite's teaching career and positions within the college.

My brother Gerald Max Thorp (deceased), the *real* writer in the family, who would be pleased that the tapes are finally transcribed, and who always encouraged me in literary endeavors.

My brother Victor George Thorp and his wife, Carmen, for their patience with my questions. Their memories were frequently essential in verifying statements in the text.

My nephew, Gordon Thorp, for his part in providing scans of family photographs.

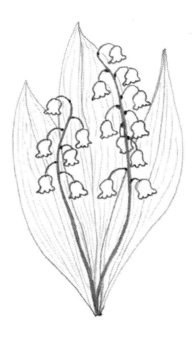

Introduction

On a pleasant May weekend in 1978, Augusta Pflug Thorp celebrated her eighty-ninth birthday with her family at her home on Black Creek in Clay County, Florida, where she had lived since the spring of 1911. Shortly after the occasion, my brother Victor suggested that it would be a good idea to record some of her memories for future generations, so I arranged to spend a few days with her that summer with my tape recorder. During the three days I was there, we were alone, so we were able to talk without interruption or distraction. Many of those conversations were taped, and many were recorded on notepads. It was a wonderful, rewarding time for me, since we had not been able to visit in such a close and private way for many years.

In transcribing the audiotapes of our conversations and the notes that I took when the recorder was not running, I have tried to keep the relaxed tone of that time and have edited passages only where necessary for the meaning to be clear. I have left out parts of the conversations that referred to unrelated topics or passages that contained distracting repetitions or false starts. We allowed the conversations to ramble because that's the way memories come. I regret that there were not more tapes and notes, and there are so very many things I wish I had asked but didn't think of until it was too late, but that's always the way of it. I wish I could have stayed there for the entire summer to record a fuller history. Throughout the manuscript, there are italicized comments by Victor and me following some of the passages. These comments, added long after the interviews, serve to explain or add to the information in the statements they follow. I regret that I was not able to include information contributed by Gerald, also, but he left us too soon.

A multitude of questions arise. For example: Considering Max's attitude concerning marriage for women, would Augusta and Earl have married in 1920 if Max had not died in 1919? Why had we children never heard the exciting story of Oscar's being detained as a "suspicious" person by the French government shortly before World War I (appendix 6)? Was Oscar's death really the result of an illness, or did it occur under "unusual circumstances," as Marie always suspected? What happened to cause the capsizing of the *Alert*? Was there any substance to the legend drifting around Virginia Intermont College that Marguerite had lost the only man she ever loved in World War I? And where did Otto go?

It has been a pleasure transcribing these conversations, and I hope generations that did not know Augusta or hear her narratives of country life in early twentieth-century North Florida will enjoy reading some of her experiences and opinions.

An acquaintance asked me if I considered myself qualified to write such a book. After a moment's consideration, I answered, "Yes!"

I consider myself qualified because it is my story, as well as Augusta's. No one else could present it with my affection; no one else could have studied the photos and narratives and come to the same conclusions about the characters. No one else could get to know the characters and weep for the grandparents, uncle, and brother I never had the opportunity to know and love. I lived in the slowly settling house. I experienced distant war and its effects on a patriotic population, and I longed to hear the family stories, again and again.

ALICE MARIE THORP DUXBURY
SUMMER 2014

About the Principal Characters

THE PFLUGS

Max Otto Pflug was born August 8, 1854, in Mylau, Germany. Wilhelmine Ernestine Henriette Laura Johanna Marie Fischer was born January 13, 1868, in Schneverdingen, Germany. Max and Marie married on June 18, 1888, in Prague, Austria. At the age of thirteen, Marie had told her parents that Max was the man she would marry, even though he was thirteen years older than she. Strangely, Marie was superstitious about the number thirteen.

Max and Marie had three children: Dora Marie Victoria (Augusta), born in Berlin, Germany, on May 21, 1889; Laura Rosa Louise Margarethe (Marguerite), born in Prague, Austria, on April 26, 1891; and Max Otto Heinrich Wilhelm Constantine (Oscar), born in Prague, Bohemia, on June 11, 1892. In 1898, Max brought his family to the United States and settled in Newark, New Jersey, where he took a position with the *Robinson-Roders* [*Roeders*] Company, described by the Greater New York Merchants' Association in New York as "a combination of the largest and oldest feather factories in the world, viz: that of William H. Robinson, established in Brooklyn twenty-five years ago, and that of August Roders, established in Berlin, Germany, 1790."

The children, already fluent in English from their schooling in Germany and Switzerland, quickly adjusted to life in the United States. Augusta remarked that she was surprised how much more she had learned about American history, geography, states, capitals, and grammar than her American-born classmates in New Jersey.

Max did not hide his disappointment that his first two children were girls, even to the point of insisting that Augusta have a boy's haircut at least once when she was very young. Augusta felt that Marguerite attempted to compensate for his disappointment with her very competitive nature.

Max's insistence that his daughters should become educated and have careers, however, served them well.

Otto Pflug, Max's nephew, came to Florida in January 1911 to find land that might provide a good location for a plant nursery and also serve as a retirement home for Max, then in his fifty-seventh year. After looking at several properties, Otto decided on the present Black Creek property, consisting of thirty acres with six hundred feet of waterfront on Black Creek, a navigable tributary of the Saint Johns River.

On Friday, April 7, 1911, Max, Marie, and twenty-one-year-old Augusta arrived in Jacksonville, Florida, having come by steamer from New York, a three days' journey. Marguerite and Oscar remained behind, she in Montclair Normal School and he at work. The first day in their new home was Palm Sunday, April 9, 1911. Augusta said that her first impression of the area, as they traveled down Black Creek from Jacksonville in a passenger boat, was its "greenness." That greenness betrayed them, however, when, in the summer before their first Christmas in their new home, Augusta and Marguerite chose a lovely small cypress tree near the Creek to be their Christmas tree. When they returned for it in December, true to its deciduous nature, it had dropped all its leaves.

The family's furniture had been shipped by rail to nearby Russell, where it was unloaded from the railroad car, which it filled to capacity, into a horse-drawn wagon and transported to their new home, requiring several trips and the assistance of the sturdy hired helper who owned the wagon.

In June 1911, Marguerite arrived and soon after registered at Stetson University in DeLand, Florida, from which she graduated in 1914. Then, with glowing recommendations from the president of Stetson, she taught German and French at Virginia Intermont College in Bristol, Virginia, from 1914 until her retirement in 1957. After retirement, she taught French, German, and Latin at King College, in Bristol, Tennessee, as an adjunct professor, until 1970. Marguerite, often referred to in this text as "Auntie," did not marry. The demand for her teaching skills resulted in an entertaining exchange of academically frosty letters between the president of Stetson and the president of Virginia Intermont, just two years after her graduation from Stetson, when both institutions were vying for her presence on their faculties (appendix 5).

Oscar served in the US Army during World War I, enlisting in 1918. Having had previous training in strict military schools, Oscar achieved the rank of second lieutenant. He left the army in 1920, after which he was employed by the Vacuum Oil Company as an export manager and lived in New York, marrying Ann Evers in 1921. Oscar and Ann had one son, Robert (Bobby) W. Pflug, born May 3, 1922.

Otto's effort to create a nursery was unsuccessful, as were other attempts to farm on the property, possibly because of the family's unfamiliarity with farming. Crops attempted included corn, rice, tomatoes, and potatoes. Even Max's pecan grove failed to prosper, producing a marketable crop only in 1931. Otto surreptitiously left by train one Sunday afternoon and was never heard from again. After Max's death in 1919, farming was abandoned.

Augusta began teaching in Highland School in Bradford County, Florida, in 1911, with fifteen pupils in a one-room school. In the course of her career, Augusta taught in other schools in Duval, Clay, and Bradford counties. Among those were Spring Glen (Duval), East Jacksonville (Duval), Ortega (Duval), Pine Grove (Clay), Middleburg (Clay), Doctors Inlet (Clay), Brooker (Bradford), Orange Park (Clay), and Penney Farms (Clay), until her retirement in 1952. Augusta served as principal at both Doctors Inlet School in the 1920s and Orange Park School in the 1930s. Neither Augusta nor Marguerite missed a day of classes in their entire teaching careers because of illness. Augusta took time off only for the births and care of her children.

THE THORPS

George Washington Thorp was born December 2, 1848, in Lebanon, Kentucky. Jane Ball was born November 17, 1856, in Hanging Rock, Ohio. George and Jane married on July 2, 1871, in Seneca, Missouri.

George and Jane had five children: Alonzo, born April 22, 1872, in Seneca, Missouri; Frances Ann (Fanny), born November 22, 1874, in Joplin, Missouri; Margaret May (Maggie), born January 14, 1878, in Wellington, Kansas; *Wilbur* Gordon, born July 28, 1881, in Wellington, Kansas (appendix 7); and Robert (Earl), born November 28, 1883, in Seneca, Missouri. The Thorps—father, mother, and Earl—moved to Florida in 1916 from Conway Springs, Kansas, and, after a land exchange, settled on eighty acres in the area now known as Lake Asbury. Frances married in 1894, and Margaret married in 1904. Earl was proud of his mixed ancestry that included Scots, English, and Native American.

Earl and Augusta met through his family's acquaintance with Max Pflug, for whom George ground corn at his mill. Earl served in the US Army in the Philippine Insurrection in 1901 and 1902, where he suffered a serious head injury that caused him frequent, debilitating headaches for the remainder of his life. He served aboard the sailing ship *Astral* in 1903, and on other sailing ships in the interim, until he enlisted in the US Naval Reserve Force as machinist's mate second class on February 1, 1918. When the war ended, Earl volunteered with Herbert Hoover's ARA (American Relief Administration) in Europe in 1919. On September 30, 1921, he was issued an honorable discharge as blacksmith first class from the Seventh Naval District. From 1921 to 1942, he worked from home repairing autos, doing metal work, welding, and carpentry, and employing other skills he had learned in his father's blacksmith shop in Conway Springs, Kansas. From early 1942 to the end of 1944, he worked in the shipyard at Pearl Harbor, Hawaii, with the civil service.

Earl and Augusta married on June 19, 1920, in a civil ceremony in Jacksonville, Florida, with Marie and Marguerite as their witnesses.

BIRTHS

On April 12, 1922, Augusta gave birth to a stillborn child whom she and Earl named Hugh Gordon. Subsequently, Augusta gave birth successfully on September 25, 1923, to Victor George, on October 24, 1927, to

Gerald Max, and on December 19, 1931, to Alice Marie. All were born in Jacksonville, Florida, at Riverside Hospital.

DEATHS

Max Pflug died peacefully on March 16, 1919, at home, of "heart dropsy" (chronic heart failure). As he was dying, Max told those around him that he was hearing beautiful music.

Hugh Gordon Thorp was stillborn April 2, 1922.

Jane Thorp died August 20, 1927 in Farmington, Michigan.

Oscar Pflug died on June 11, 1929, in Kobe, Japan, where he was representing the Vacuum Oil Company in the Orient.

George Washington Thorp died November 29, 1932, in Pontiac, Michigan.

Marie Pflug died June 8, 1946, at her Florida home, after suffering multiple strokes over a period of several years.

Earl Thorp died January 16, 1961, of a pulmonary embolism after colon surgery in Clay Memorial Hospital in Green Cove Springs, Florida.

Marguerite Pflug died August 13, 1972, in Memorial Hospital in Bristol, Tennessee, after several strokes.

Augusta Pflug Thorp died November 19, 1981, in Orange Park, Florida, of age-related natural causes.

Gerald Thorp died May 1, 1983, in Gainesville, Florida, from injuries in a traffic collision caused by an inebriated driver.

Robert Pflug, Oscar's son, died May 5, 1999, in West Islip, New York.

Max, Hugh Gordon, Marie, Earl, Marguerite, Augusta, and Gerald are buried in Oakland Cemetery (formerly Pine Grove Cemetery) in the family plot under the large oak chosen by Max. Oscar is listed in the family Bible as having been interred in Cypress Hill National Cemetery, a military cemetery on Long Island.

Alphabetical Characters at a Glance

Pflug, Marguerite, 1891–1972: Augusta's sister

Pflug, Marie Fischer, 1868–1946: Augusta's mother

Pflug, Max, 1854–1919: Augusta's father

Pflug, Oscar, 1892–1929: Augusta's brother

Pflug, Robert W. (Bobby), 1922–1999: Augusta's nephew, Oscar's son

Thorp, Alice Marie, 1931: Augusta's daughter

Thorp, Augusta Pflug, 1889–1981

Thorp, George Washington, 1848–1932: Augusta's father-in-law, Earl's father

Thorp, Gerald Max, 1927–1983: Augusta's third son

Thorp, Hugh Gordon, 1922 (stillborn): Augusta's first son

Thorp, Jane Ball, 1856–1927: Augusta's mother-in-law, Earl's mother

Thorp, Robert Earl, 1883–1961: Augusta's husband

Thorp, Victor George, 1923: Augusta's second son

Chronological Characters at a Glance

Thorp, George Washington, 1848–1932: Augusta's father-in-law

Pflug, Max, 1854–1919: Augusta's father

Thorp, Jane Ball, 1856–1927: Augusta's mother-in-law

Pflug, Marie, 1868–1946: Augusta's mother

Thorp, Robert Earl, 1883–1961: Augusta's husband

Thorp, Augusta Pflug, 1889–1981

Pflug, Marguerite, 1891–1972: Augusta's sister

Pflug, Oscar, 1892–1929: Augusta's brother

Pflug, Robert W. (Bobby) 1922–1999: Augusta's nephew, Oscar's son

Thorp, Hugh Gordon, 1922 (stillborn): Augusta's first son

Thorp, Victor George, 1923: Augusta's second son

Thorp, Gerald Max, 1927–1983: Augusta's third son

Thorp, Alice Marie, 1931: Augusta's daughter

CHAPTER 1

The Story of a House—
Man Proposes, Cryptotermes
Cavifrons Disposes

In its early years, it was a charming example of a southern country home. It was not a pillared mansion with balconies and sweeping lawns with peacocks but simply a typical, humble but gracious Florida home. It was built with strong materials: Dade County pine planks, inside and out, and a classic brick chimney painted white—the color of the house.

Southeast view of house

The house was graced on the south and east sides by an open porch, and on the north side by a screened porch. It stood straight and strong in the midst of a clearing surrounded by woods, its upright log foundations modestly concealed by panels of white lattice. The house did not know how rudely those log foundations would betray it.

Downstairs there were four rooms: kitchen, bedroom, dining room, and parlor (which was what such a room was called in 1911).

The kitchen, on the west side of the house, was equipped with a kerosene stove, a large work table, shelves, cabinets, and a freestanding food safe, its doors covered by metal screen to foil ants and other insects. An entry door opened onto the south porch, and one window on the west side of the room provided a lovely view of a sturdy, young hickory tree, which gave pleasant, deep shade on summer days and promised, for the future, one low branch perfect for a child's swing and other strong branches for children to climb. A hand pump supplied water for the kitchen, and a kerosene lamp attached to the west wall provided illumination.

Northeast view, screened porch

The bedroom, also on the west side of the house immediately north of the kitchen, served many purposes in its time, from bedroom to den, to playroom, to storage room, to children's library. It was small and contained one closet and a window on its west side.

The dining room, east of the kitchen, contained the fireplace, the only built-in source of heat on cold winter days. Several feet from the fireplace was a window on the south end of the room, in front of which sat a Victrola on a small, round table.

An Aladdin kerosene lamp hung over the dining room table, which served as meal table, sewing table, study table, conference table, reading table, writing table, or game table, depending upon the family's wishes or needs.

On the west side of the dining room, wooden stairs ascended to the upstairs bedrooms. On the north side of the dining room was a door to the parlor, open in warm weather, closed in cold weather. Over the door to the parlor was a wooden plaque that read, in translation from the German script, "In the new home, the old blessing."

Augusta playing the Victrola

On the northwest side was the doorway to the kitchen. Underneath the stairs was a scary, dark, commodious closet. When the house timbers gently shifted in the night, as timbers will do in a wood frame house, things would randomly fall from shelves in the closet, and sometimes a beautifully carved music box stored in the closet would be startled into playing its sad German melody, "Ich hatt' einen Kameraden" (a German song mourning a comrade lost in battle). Other times, something, perhaps tiny mouse toes, would disturb the strings of a mandolin on a shelf near the music box.

On the east side of the dining room, there was one window with a view of the yard and trees and whatever might be blooming, according to the season.

The parlor held a piano, dozens of shelved books, and two horsehair sofas for brief, uncomfortable reading times, such as doing research in one of the encyclopedias. On the east side of the parlor were the front door and one window. Another window on the north side opened onto the north screened porch, closed in to serve as a "sleeping porch" in 1946.

Marie and Max's tribute to Oscar

Various comfortable chairs, suitable for longer, more comfortable reading times, occupied places along the walls. A dark, ornately carved, octagonal table with lions' heads and paws carved onto its single pedestal graced the center of the room. Another small table stood by the door.

On the north wall was a large painting of a boy with a Saint Bernard dog, and on the west wall was an even larger painting of the beautiful Koenigsee, the Bavarian lake, site of Neuschwanstein Castle and refuge for Mad King Ludwig.

Upstairs were two bedrooms. One had a window facing south and a dormer window facing east. The dormer window was perfectly designed to sit beside on a late summer night to look at the moon and listen to the chuck-will's-widows calling, and the owls hooting, and often to hear a lonely midnight train whistle from a distance far to the east. That bedroom had no west window, thus, unfortunately, no cooling cross-ventilation.

Like the south bedroom, the north bedroom had one dormer window facing east but another window facing north. It also had no window on the west to provide cross-ventilation. Day and night, summer heat sat stubbornly in those rooms. Each bedroom held beds with moss-filled mattresses of intense, punishing firmness. The shifting timbers would often cause the closet door of the north bedroom to swing open eerily in the night, but that was only mischief, never a threat. A large steamer trunk against the west wall held carefully packed fine bone china, silverware, and embroidered linens, too "good" to use in a house that held active children.

In its early years, it was a fine house, a house to be admired—straight, tall, and strong. Then the termites found it—never consuming the solid heart pine boards of the house but eagerly eating the untreated log sections that served as its foundations.

They ate and multiplied, and the house discovered that its strong supports from below were beginning to crumble upon themselves. It happened so slowly that no one at first was aware of the disintegration. Then things began to shift.

Over a period of about forty years, the westerly settling slowly continued until the slant of the house could be clearly perceived in a cup of coffee, bowl of soup, or boat of gravy. A marble or ball dropped on the floor of the house rolled always to the west. As the foundation started to crumble, its unevenness caused the walls of the house to sigh sad sounds as they began to twist on their frames. By the 1940s, light could be seen of a morning at the juncture of the south and east walls in the south bedroom, but the house still loyally remained upright.

"Equinoctial storms" (now known as tropical depressions, tropical storms, or hurricanes, depending upon their ferocity) came frequently. During one of the storms in 1944, the family watched as the now venerable old hickory tree immediately west of the house fought bravely against the battering winds from the east that strained the timbers of the house and forced the hickory to bow. The last hard gust from the east snapped the sturdy trunk of the old hickory, and down it crashed toward the west, safely away from the vulnerable roof of the house and into the quiet center of the storm. When the center passed, and the winds blew hard from the west, the old house had been spared disaster and still stood, perhaps leaning a bit more to the west and missing the companionship of its old friend.

Another year, lightning struck a huge oak tree and raced along a wire radio aerial to the part of the eaves where the aerial entered the house. The roof caught fire, the family sought help, neighbors came, and the fire was extinguished, but the roof of the kitchen did not survive. The house had to suffer the humiliation of galvanized roofing sheets over the kitchen.

As time passed, the music box still played in the night, closet doors more frequently opened unexpectedly, and life went on.

In the 1940s, running water from an artesian well was provided, and electrical wires snaked around interior walls to provide electricity. The kitchen then held a refrigerator, a water heater provided hot water, and food was prepared on an electric stove.

One generation died, and a second and a third generation grew and thrived. The house saw many loved pets romping through the years and shared the happiness of life and the grief of loss. It saw hardship, and still its threatened walls and joints held strong. It saw two stars on its front door, the outside door to the parlor, where anyone who came to visit would see them, displayed with pride for two sons in military service, one in the US Navy and one in the US Marines. It served as a compassionate vessel for joy, sorrow, fun, loss, learning, camaraderie, and love.

In the late 1950s, the house saw the construction of a smaller house, built on concrete foundations, immediately north of its porches. The old house had been declared to be unsafe for the two remaining members of the second generation who still lived there. Before the new house was completed, one of those two was gone, leaving only the remaining member of the second generation to move into the new, small house, alone. By then, all the members of the third generation lived elsewhere, so the old house stood alone and still, a haven for wasps, dust, and memories.

But the ending was not entirely sad. A neighbor expressed interest in the solid pine boards of the old house. An agreement was reached, and the neighbor, with his helpers, took those boards, cleared away the remainder of the old house, and built a new house of his own, not far away.

Cleaning up

So the old house lived on, at least in part, to see other generations live and grow. The music box on its steady shelf in the new, small house played no more nocturnal tricks and sang its sad song only when it was asked to sing.

Augusta says good-bye to the old house—1967

Alice Marie Thorp Duxbury

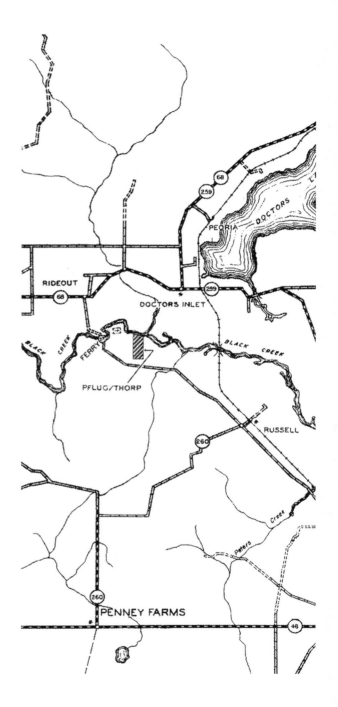

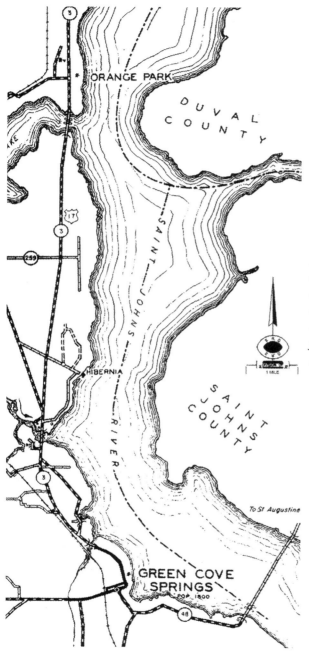

Eastern Clay County, Florida, as it was in the late nineteenth and early twentieth centuries (Copyright 2015 by Mark Thorp Duxbury. Based on and derived from State of Florida State Road Department 1936 original.)

CHAPTER 2

Conversations with Augusta— Three Days in June 1978

Alice: When you first started teaching, how did students get to school if they didn't live nearby? Was there any sort of school bus?

Augusta: When I first started teaching in Highland School in 1911, there were about a dozen one-room schools, grades one through eight, and only one high school in Clay County. As far as school buses were concerned, the one I'm thinking of now was quite a large donkey-drawn wagon that they had for transporting children to school. Otherwise, children had to live close by a school or be transported by their families.

School bus in Spring Glen

Alice: Did the person that owned the donkey do that just to help, or was the county paying them for it, or—

Augusta: Yes, somebody owned the donkey, but the county paid for the use of it.

Alice: Where was that?

Augusta: That was in Spring Glen.

Alice: I guess it wouldn't have been practical to have horse or mule or donkey-drawn transportation out here.

Augusta: Oh, no. It couldn't have been here. It was over there in Spring Glen—but I just can't remember the year exactly.

Alice: It must have been after 1911 when you first started teaching, and you were married in 1920 when you were teaching in Ortega, you said. So it was earlier than that.

Augusta: Yes, that would have been before the 1920s.

Alice: And then Victor was born in 1923, so it had to be—

Augusta: It must have been in the "teens" then, 1916 or so.

Alice: As far as any other transportation, I suppose they didn't really have any motorized school buses until later than that?

Augusta: Those were much later, because, you see, that had to be when there were more cars, too. At the time of which I'm speaking, there was hardly anyone in the county who had a car, even.

Alice: While we're talking about schools, they still had such subjects as Latin in school then, didn't they?

Augusta: Well, they taught very little Latin. I think Lillian Watkins could teach some Latin and math.

Alice: Yes, she was teaching Latin and math when I was in Clay High School. Our Latin and algebra classes were very small, only five or six pupils, I think.

Augusta: So you see that would be when Latin and higher math were still being taught—I mean *already* being taught to a certain extent and—what was it now you wanted to know?

Alice: I was curious about what kinds of courses they did have for the country kids. You know, it doesn't really seem practical to have Latin and—

Augusta: Well, no one was compelled to take them. They could graduate from high school without taking those. I don't even know exactly what they had in physics or anything like that.

Alice: I guess—nothing. I don't remember anything like that when I was in school. The highest math classes in Clay High School when I was there were geometry and algebra II.

Augusta: I think possibly what you remember is about what they had before.

Alice: Another thing that I think would be very interesting is what salaries were then. During the Depression, you worked for nothing sometimes, didn't you?

Augusta: We often had to wait for our checks. You might put that when I started to teach—that was in 1911—the salary was about forty dollars a month.

Alice: And do you remember what you were making when you retired in the 1950s?

Augusta: Yes, when I retired in 1952—of course that was in this county, with probably less than in other counties, because Clay County was always one of the poorer counties—I was making about $190 a month.

Alice: Even for my part-time teaching in Palm Beach County, just six hours a week, I was getting $163 a month, and that's a lot less than the full-time teachers were making. (*Alice: This* was *in the 1970s.*)

Augusta: I know that when I was teaching—up to 1952—I never received over two hundred dollars. I don't think I made even two hundred dollars a month. After deductions, it was something like $190-something. *(Alice: According to payroll records from the Clay County School District Human Resources Department, in 1942 Augusta was making $106.05 a month. When she retired in 1952, she was earning $290.00 a month, before deductions.)*

Alice: And during the Depression, you were sometimes paid in "scrip"? *(Alice: "Scrip" refers to notes that promised payment when money became available.)*

Augusta: Yes, and then for months, we teachers just got that and had to wait until it could be cashed. For months, really, we didn't get any money.

Alice: Then how did people live?

Augusta: Well, everybody had to get groceries. We had a big bill outstanding at Morgan's grocery store in Orange Park in the thirties, which we paid off over time. And, of course, when your father was here, he made something off and on. He was always making repairs for people. People would bring cars to repair. You may remember that.

Alice: Yes, I do.

Augusta: It was a little something. Of course, he couldn't charge very much in those days. I have no idea how much he would charge for what job. That was his business, but that was what we had—what I made, what he could make. And let's see, the boys at that time were too young to be working.

Alice: Gerald worked at Lee Field (Green Cove Springs Naval Base) during the forties.

Augusta: That was later then.

Alice: Yes, it was when Victor was in the service, but I remember that when we were living in Orange Park, in the thirties, Victor worked a little bit. Was it at Giessen's Poultry Farm? *(Victor: Yes, at fifteen cents an hour.)*

Augusta: Yes. And I'll tell you something else. You know, even though Victor was in the navy with a very small salary in the forties, he would always send something home.

Alice: I remember that.

Augusta: Then it was what little I got, what little your dad got, and what Victor could send. And that made your grandma so happy. You know he had ten dollars made over to her every month from his salary, and she was so pleased. Of course, ten dollars meant much more in those days. It wasn't that the amount pleased her so much but the fact that he thought of her and had that sent to her. She was so pleased about Victor's doing that. I was glad he did. She had done a lot with you children. She helped me a lot more than I realized at the time. I can now see how much she helped. She'd have meals ready. I'd come home from school, and she'd have supper all cooked.

Alice: I can remember the time after that when she was so sick, and she couldn't do anything like that anymore. You would come home from school in the evening, and I could never understand why you didn't get right out of the car and come into the house. You'd just sit there for a few minutes, but I understand that now. It was a period of rest and quiet before you had to come in and take over everything else. That must have been hard. I also remember that you would often fall asleep at the supper table. You must have been exhausted.

Augusta: Well, that was so hard with my mother because she just couldn't stand colored people around. We could have gotten a colored woman to come here and stay with her for a reasonable amount—or what would have seemed reasonable at the time. Not very much, but it would have been something. But my mother wouldn't have a colored person, and it was very hard to get anybody else whom we could have been able to pay. We couldn't have been able to pay very much.

Mrs. Owens came for a while for a dollar a day. But now, remember that she drove here, and it would take some gas, even if gas wasn't so expensive as it is now. Now she couldn't possibly do it without paying more for gas than she was making. One dollar a day, and she would be driving with her own car and gas. She couldn't do that very long, you know. Her folks told her it just wouldn't pay for her to do that. Now, if we had just been closer to where the Owens lived, but it was too far to walk, and it was hard in those days that my mother was particular about who was with her and wouldn't stay alone. I mean, even if we left her for a short time, she wouldn't like it. For instance, if she was in bed then, like she was much of the time, and somebody who was staying with her would go outside to do something else, she didn't like that. "No! Come right back in again and stay with me!" And she always had the idea that she saw things in dark corners. Do you remember? She'd insist there was somebody standing in the corner or something. And that's what made her so terribly difficult. Her eyes were not good at all.

Alice: Yes, I can remember that. Once when I was staying with her, she saw the yucca plant—the spanish bayonet—that was blooming in the pecan grove. She was sure there was someone standing down in the grove, and I couldn't convince her otherwise. I'm sure her eyes were quite bad by then.

Back to the Depression time then. I imagine there weren't very many kids in school anyway. Did you have compulsory education? When did that start?

Augusta: Oh, goodness, compulsory education—that was much later. You know they still had some colored schools, but many of the children just wouldn't go. Or else they had teachers who couldn't teach them anything because most of the colored people couldn't even read in those days. They didn't really have a chance to learn.

Alice: I'll have to look that up. I'm not sure when compulsory education began.

Augusta: That was really quite a bit later, I think. *(Alice: It was 1915 in Florida but probably not sternly enforced in rural areas.)*

Alice: I remember hearing about truant officers for a long time, but I don't know if that was in individual states or whether they could enforce attendance or not. Remember in *Huckleberry Finn* and *Tom Sawyer*?

Augusta: Yes, I remember that.

Alice: They tried to make Huckleberry go to school, and he didn't want to?

Augusta: No, in those days—I mean those days way back then—no one was forced to go. You were given the opportunity, and if you didn't avail yourself of it, you just didn't go. That's all there was to it.

Alice: What I was thinking of is that the child labor laws were a lot more lenient then, too, and I imagine a lot of those kids had to be out working.

Augusta: Well, I guess they were. Some of them were probably needed at home. And I know school would start—now that might be interesting—many of these little schools would start in July and close in January. They had about six months between July and January, and that was because the strawberries would ripen then. Other crops would ripen in January, too, but it was mostly the strawberries for which they needed the children for the picking. They couldn't afford to hire anyone to pick because the strawberries didn't sell at too high a price.

But, anyway, that was the reason that in 1932, when you were a baby, we went to Brooker in July. I think it was right after the Fourth of July holiday. And we were in Brooker then until after Christmas. But that was the reason—because the children were needed early in the year—in January and February—for picking strawberries or whatever else was ripening at that time. And nobody could afford to pay for anything like that and still make any kind of a profit. If they had hired someone for pay, they probably would have paid out more than they could have gotten for their fruit.

Alice: And strawberries were such an ephemeral crop, too. They had to get them right to the market.

Augusta: I know that year I thought it was terrible to start school in July and then teach all through the hot season.

Alice: And no air-conditioning!

Augusta: Oh, no. Open windows—that was all.

Now let me see if there was anything else about the schools then. They were just so different then from what they are now.

Alice: Another thing that would be interesting would be how the teachers were chosen. They weren't necessarily required to have degrees then, were they? Would you explain about that?

Augusta: There were teachers' examinations given in Green Cove Springs at the courthouse. There were separate examinations in arithmetic, geography, and so on, not different questions on different subjects in the same examination.

We usually had to go for several days to take those examinations and then—now this was something, too, that was ridiculous—they would choose people whom they thought sufficiently well educated to make the corrections. One year Auntie was chosen—she was here on a vacation— and when the examinations came in, they asked her to help correct them. The names were not on our papers—we each had a number because they didn't want anyone to be partial—but the funny thing was that Auntie knew my handwriting. I think there were three of them correcting—and Auntie would pick out what she knew was my paper.

Alice: That would be an easy one to correct!

Augusta: And I could do better than most of them, simply because I had had the opportunity of a better education in the schools that we had attended. She said that when she looked at some other papers, mine was so much better, and she had no difficulty reading it because she could read my handwriting well.

At that time, if you took an examination, you were classified as a first-grade teacher or a second-grade teacher or a third-grade teacher.

Alice: They didn't mean school grade by "grade," did they? They didn't mean the first-grade teacher taught the first grade?

Augusta: No, it just meant "rank." If you were a "first-grade" teacher, you were a first-class teacher.

Alice: How did they determine where to send the teachers, then?

Augusta: Of course, some of them did manage to get jobs in other counties sometimes, if they had done fairly well. Those certificates were good, if I remember correctly, just for one year. You had to take the examinations regularly so that they knew you weren't forgetting everything. And if you made an average of over 90 percent within five years of exams, then you got a life certificate. Sometime I must show you my life certificate. It's ridiculous—I *still* have a life certificate. It doesn't say anything like you have to quit at ninety or when. It doesn't say anything about retiring because, at that time, there were no teachers' pensions. Please remark about that, too—*no teacher pensions!*

Alice: When you quit, you had no income.

Augusta: Then you had no income. And some teachers were getting so old that they couldn't teach well anymore. I think I have mentioned old Mrs. Richardson in Jacksonville. I was teaching in East Jacksonville at the East Jacksonville School one of my first years in Florida. Of course, East Jacksonville School is a big school now and was then even. Poor Mrs. Richardson was a widow. She seemed to have no family—no children or grandchildren—and she was getting very old. She must have been up in her seventies, and she was getting so that she really wanted to quit teaching, but she couldn't because she had no income at all. She seemed to have no one who would help her, no relatives or anyone.

Alice: That's sad.

Augusta: Awfully sad. And she finally, then, taught until she got sick and died. I know I used to feel so sorry for her. She had been, for those days, a good teacher. She just simply could not retire. There wasn't anything in the way of what people have now, like social security, pensions, and everything. A woman called me the other day from a government agency checking up on old people. When she asked me with what I was not satisfied, I said

I was well satisfied, and I told her that we old people are better off now than ever before, with social security and pensions and so on. *(Alice: Social Security passed in 1935. Teachers' pensions in Florida went into effect July 1, 1939. So Augusta was probably better paid in retirement than in her many years of teaching.)*

Alice: You probably messed up all their records.

Augusta: You say *I* messed up all their records? They probably didn't even put that down.

Alice: They probably said, "This one's crazy. We'll just forget about her."

Augusta: I know she sounded surprised. I said, "I'm satisfied, really. I have no complaint." She said, *"Really?* You have *no* complaint?"

Alice: And that messed up everything. You can be sure the others she contacted had *lots* of complaints! And I remember another time you probably messed up the records—when the officer came out to tell you he had to take your driver's license after you had been in to renew it. You handed it over without any complaint, saying you knew you couldn't really see well enough anymore to be a safe driver. You told me he was astonished and asked if you weren't going to get angry and argue and yell at him. He was so surprised, because he said that's what most people did.

Well, after you averaged your 90 percent or above for those five years, did you have to keep on taking the exams?

Augusta: No. Then I had my life certificate—and I still have it. That's the funny thing, you know. I have the life certificate, which I suppose would mean—but, no, they wouldn't take me now, of course, for other reasons even than my eyes, you know. I couldn't possibly teach now. *(Alice: Augusta developed macular degeneration in her later years.)*

But I do have it, and I want to show it to you sometime when I can get to it. I haven't looked at it now for many years, but it was always amusing to me in years past when once in a while I'd look at it. My goodness! I can teach all my life! I didn't think then of my eyes getting really bad. I couldn't teach anything now. I would have to see to do any teaching. I would have to see what was in the book or what a pupil was doing with writing. It would all have to be oral. I suppose one thing I could be teaching is German. If anybody wanted to know German, I could talk to him without having anything written down. Yes, I got my life certificate and still have it.

Alice: And yet, even with your life certificate they required you to go back and take courses when you started teaching again in the forties after Grandma died? You went back to Gainesville, I remember.

Augusta: The reason I did that is because I didn't have a degree from a college. I wanted a college degree.

Alice: Oh—for the pay? The pay was better, wasn't it?

Augusta: No, because it would have *looked* a whole lot better. It looked kind of strange that way—you know, a life certificate, and I didn't even have a college degree. I do have—I must show those to you—I took so many courses that I think I had enough to have a degree, but I don't know just how many of those correspondence courses would count toward a college degree.

Alice: Yes, they're particular about that.

Augusta: So I haven't even messed with it now because that's all in the past. It isn't that I didn't really work enough toward a degree with all of those courses that I took. You know, every summer I'd even go to Gainesville and stay there a while to take classes. You remember that.

Alice: Yes, I remember.

Augusta: You know Grandma died in 1946, and you were there with me.

Alice: No, that was when we were in Tallahassee (Florida State College for Women). You went to Gainesville (the University of Florida) before she died. When you went to Tallahassee, I went with you. You went to

Gainesville when I was younger. One time was the year that Victor went into the service.

Augusta: When we were renting in Tallahassee, you and I, I had tried to get a room in a dormitory, but they wouldn't let you come in with me. They couldn't take anybody who wasn't a student. Do you remember being with me up on the hill on College Avenue? Whose house was that?

Alice: Yes, I remember. That was Mrs. Walker's house. Mrs. Walker's mother, who was ninety years old that summer, taught me to sew, and I took a typing class at Lively Technical Center.

Augusta at Florida State College for Women, Tallahassee, Florida, summer 1946

Augusta: I think you were fourteen.

Alice: Yes, see that's what I was saying we were mixed up about; one of the years you went to UF was the year Victor went into the navy, in 1941.

Earl was on temporary assignment to duty on this ship, the
USS Leonidas, when he sustained his serious shoulder injury.
Photo: US Naval History & Heritage Online Library

Augusta: There was just so much in those years, you know. Let's see, when was it your dad went to Pearl Harbor?

Alice: That was early in 1942.

Augusta: Yes, when the war began. It was soon after the Japanese attacked Pearl Harbor.

Alice: It was 1942 that he went, and then he got back when?

Augusta: I don't think he got back until early 1945.

Alice: I think you're correct.

Augusta: He was gone not quite, but almost, three years.

Alice: During that time was when Grandma was bedridden.

Augusta: And then I had to give up and stay home, finally. I certainly would not have retired yet. I stayed home for three years, and you and Gerald alternated days staying with her one semester so I could finish the school year. You remember, don't you, that Grandma refused to stay anywhere away from home where someone could take care of her? In a nursing home? And then those places were very expensive, too.

Alice: Generally, Grandma was in good health though, wasn't she, until her first stroke?

Augusta: Yes, she was, except for her migraine headaches. You know, Auntie had a couple of surgeries for cancer, one when she was quite young and one much later when she was teaching in Virginia. I think she had a hysterectomy when she was young and a mastectomy when she was older. She never spoke about her health, probably because she considered a health problem to be a weakness.

It's sad that I have outlived both my younger siblings.

Alice: But you had a close brush with death yourself when you were little, didn't you?

Augusta: Yes, I had typhoid fever when I was very young, and that was extremely serious. My mother told me that when the doctor left after seeing me one morning when I was so sick, he said he really didn't expect that I would still be alive when he came back in the afternoon. I survived though. And did you know back then people believed that a person's hair sapped the body's strength, so it was usual to cut off all of a typhoid patient's hair? My hair had been wavy before it was all cut off, but it grew back straight. I think that was the only lasting effect of my typhoid fever episode.

Alice: That must have been very frightening for you and for your parents.

Speaking of health reminds me of that horrible "Rasol" medicine that Grandma made us kids drink to "stay well." Remember, Dr. Rasmussen, near Penney Farms, made it? I think it was mostly sulfur. It was very strong and tasted terrible, but I suppose it didn't do any harm. I remember, also, that many people in Clay County were sure that Dr. Rasmussen was a German spy, and he did mysteriously disappear during World War II. I think part of the suspicion was caused by that yacht that he had in his back yard near Penney Farms, with no deep water nearby. People also suspected him of being a German Bund member. (The American German Bund was an American Nazi organization whose main goal was to promote a favorable view of Nazi Germany.)

Augusta: Yes, your grandma liked him, mostly because he was someone she could speak German with. And I guess she trusted his Rasol. He was mysterious, though. I don't know what happened to him. He also advised her to drink one glass of wine every day for her health.

Alice: Well, back to early schooldays. You've told me some interesting stories about the kids you taught.

Augusta: Could you suggest one, maybe?

Alice: Yes. I was thinking back to the Robertsons. You know, their "Our Girl," and that sort of thing? And the protectiveness that they showed for one another? I remember the Greens, too. And I remember when we went to Auntie's funeral, at the cemetery the people gathered around you, people you had taught in Pine Grove School years ago. They were all talking about things you remembered well. And they thought it was so wonderful that you remembered them individually.

Augusta: I can't remember anything else now that would be interesting, but one thing I do remember was that the Robertsons had, I guess it must have been seven boys and the one girl. The number of children was not remarkable. Many families had eight or nine, maybe ten children. The Robertsons were remarkable because they had all boys except for one girl, and she was right about in the middle.

Alice: That was Carrie, wasn't it?

Augusta: Let's see. Carrie Robertson. She came here one time quite a while ago. Did I tell you about that?

Alice: No.

Augusta: A woman came, and she asked me—I didn't recognize her, of course—if I remembered Carrie Robertson. Anyway, we'll call her Carrie now because I can't think of any other name it might have been. But, anyway, I said yes, I remembered that Carrie Robertson was the girl with the many brothers who always spoke of her proudly as "Our Girl." That's what they were always saying—"That's *Our Girl*"—not only her brothers but also her father, too, very proud of his *one* girl.

She said she had a daughter living near here. So she evidently had a married daughter. I don't know if there were any grandchildren, but she said that they had moved over here and that she would be visiting her daughter, and she was going to come here again to visit with me, but she didn't, or at least I was not home when she came. It was pleasant to see her again.

Alice: You mean her daughter was living over there at Hidden Waters?

Augusta: The LaRue place. Her daughter was living in a trailer over there, so I don't know if her daughter's there still or not. You know people come in with trailers, and some of them don't stay long.

Alice: Well, I do remember Pa Robertson was the one the kids bragged about—"Pa ain't took a bath in twenty years!" Do you remember that?

Augusta: I remember that was true about somebody. Let's see—of course now when they said he hadn't taken a bath in all that time, I was wondering, because they were always going into the Creek.

Alice: I'm sure they meant in a bathtub.

Augusta: Maybe with soap and water and everything. Maybe that was a "bath."

Alice: They had that house on the corner up there in Russell, didn't they, where that little store is now? I think that was the Robertsons' house where we turned to go down to the post office.

Augusta: I think they lived there for a little while. Their home was really right there at the cemetery.

Alice: The Robertsons?

Augusta: Wait—no—those were the Greens.

Alice: I'm quite sure that was the Robertsons' house in Russell because I can remember that we always enjoyed seeing their flowers. They had geraniums and other plants and a rowboat with flowers in it. Even old chamber pots had flowers blooming in them on the porch.

Who was it that lived near here that killed the rattlesnake and expected Daddy to pay him some kind of reward for that? Daddy told him, "Oh, you've killed our pet rattlesnake," or, "You've killed Old Joe," or something like that.

Augusta: I know somebody killed something, but—

Alice: It was the same person, I think, that picked up a clothespin, handed it to Daddy, and said, "It pays to be honest."

Augusta: I just can't remember all of those people now. But I do remember "It pays to be honest"—that incident—but not exactly who it was. And I remember the other one, too.

Oh, and I also remember the time one of the young men from the neighborhood came by to see your dad about something when I was pregnant. I'm sure he meant it as a compliment when he told your daddy, "Miss Gussie sure looks good. She's fattenin' up like an old sow hog!"

Alice: That *is* funny!

I also remember something else, and I remember this personally, not just hearing about it. I remember the day a girl that married one of the Chesser boys came here to hide out from her husband. It was summer and in the middle of a thunderstorm, and you let her hide down by the Creek in the bathhouse. I think Victor and Gerald were both away in camp, and Grandma was not here. She was probably in Virginia with Auntie or in Germany. I think I was about six years old.

Augusta: Oh, now that was a kind of a crazy mix-up. That was Myrtle. Myrtle was married to one of the Chessers, but somehow she got mixed up with one of the brothers, and I think that's what made the trouble—but I can't remember just what finally happened.

Alice: I don't know either, but I can remember the incident well, because she was so upset, and I remember you wouldn't let her stay in the house because you didn't want any part of it. I certainly don't blame you for that!

Augusta: No, no. I didn't want anyone around under those circumstances. Nor any angry husband.

And one other thing, too, and I wouldn't want you to write that down, but I know I've told you about Bill Chesser's stealing your dad's suit and camera. That was so ridiculous because it was really my fault. We had never had anything stolen until then. I mean there wasn't any special care about locking up.

We were going to Jacksonville. It was your dad and my mother and I, the three of us who were living here at the time, after my father had died in 1919. We were going in the car, I think, but anyway all of us were gone that day. Oh, yes—it must have been in the car because we went across the Creek on the ferry. And you know that's when they could see the three of us leaving. I had locked everything except the kitchen door, which had a screen door in front of it on the outside. You know, like that door out there on the porch that you can hook. And I remember I hooked the screened door from the inside, locked all the other doors—we had two or three—but I did not lock the inside door where the screen door was, which, of course, was foolish of me. I just didn't do it because we had never felt that there was much danger of anyone coming in.

Well, when we came home again, we found that somebody had been in. I don't know what we noticed. I think that door was open. I mean the hook was unhooked. They got that unhooked, which I guess is easy enough to do on a screen door. You can reach in there and get at the screen and loosen the wire a little. So I'm always very careful now to close inside doors, besides using the hooks on the screened doors.

That day then, your father had all his clothes in that big closet upstairs, and he had not worn his best suit to Jacksonville because it was too hot. He didn't feel like dressing up much, and he put on a cooler, older one. But that suit of his was gone, and it was quite a new suit. Also he had a camera that he had bought in France, and it was an expensive camera for those days. He was very proud of the camera, and he liked to take pictures, and that was gone. Those were the two things gone. Not anything else was missing—or if anything else was gone, we didn't even notice it. No silverware or anything like that, which of course we had, nor any of the porcelain. It looked very much like some *man* taking things. And then we found out that Bill Chesser had left that very day, that afternoon, before we even got back home. He had left to take a job somewhere else—I don't remember now where. But, anyway, he was gone, and whoever had seen him told us just how he was dressed, and it was that suit of my husband's, and of course he must have taken the camera, too.

Alice: He probably sold the camera.

Augusta: Because that was right there, too. Oh, I'm sure he could get good money for it because it was a camera of which your father was very proud. And I'm very sorry about that. The camera even more than the suit, although the suit was a loss, too—almost a new suit. And since then I am careful not to consider a hooked screen door to be "locking." When we go away, I try to make sure that the inner doors are locked, too. But I know I have really felt the guilty one for that, because if I had just locked that inner door, I don't believe someone would have broken anything noticeable to get in.

Alice: He might have gotten in anyway. He *would* have gotten in some way.

Augusta: He might have gotten in. Anyway, that's what happened. Those are the only things I know of that ever were stolen from here. Of course, I may be mistaken. Other things might have been stolen, and I didn't even know it.

Alice: Also, there was the case of that dress that someone borrowed from Daddy's mother but never returned. I remember that story, too. Someone borrowed it for a funeral, didn't she? A black dress? From Daddy's mother?

Augusta: Well, she probably did. I don't even quite remember that.

Alice: And then she never did give it back.

Augusta: But I wouldn't be surprised. I don't remember that. That didn't make much impression on me, I guess. But I can readily believe that someone would borrow something and not return it.

Alice: Well, just in a haphazard way, we've gotten up to the forties. We can go back and fill in things here, if we want to, but in the forties, the first thing is the war.

Augusta: Then, of course, you remember some of that from what you've heard, I guess.

Alice: I remember quite a bit of it firsthand, too. Victor graduated in '41, didn't he?

Augusta: Yes.

Alice: And then he went into service that summer.

Augusta: That summer, and December 7, 1941, was the Japanese attack on Pearl Harbor. You may remember being up there at the gate to tell me when I came home from school that day—

Alice: I remember it happened on a Sunday, and Grandma and I heard it on the radio that evening.

Augusta: Yes, but I mean later, after the attack on Pearl Harbor, when you had a letter from Victor that they wouldn't let anybody go home for Christmas or leave the base at Norfolk.

Alice: Oh, of course!

Augusta: Well, anyway, you were at the gate, I remember. You and somebody with you—and the first thing you told me was, "Victor can't come home for Christmas," and we were all so disappointed. The attack was the seventh of December, very near to Christmas; and they had issued that order that nobody could leave the base and be away farther than forty miles, so of course it would have been too far for Victor to come here. He couldn't come home, and he said he'd already had his suitcase packed. He was so disappointed. I know we were, because it was his first Christmas away from home, so I guess all of us remember that. I remember how you were up there, and the first thing you told me was, "Victor can't come. Victor can't come."

Alice: I guess it was a while before he got home. About the next summer, probably.

How about the gasoline rationing? I remember that there were A stickers, B stickers, and C stickers for the car windshields, and you got a C sticker because you were a teacher and had to drive quite a distance to get to school.

Augusta: Yes, I could get gasoline because I was teaching.

Alice: I think the A sticker was the one that got the least, wasn't it? *(Victor: Yes.)*

Augusta: Probably. I don't even remember whether I had A, B, or "C." I do remember that not everybody could get gasoline.

Alice: We had ration tickets, didn't we, for meat?

Augusta: They were for all kinds of food—yes. It was not only meat. We were limited on certain things.

Alice: It was meat, sugar—and many, many other things.

Augusta: I don't remember what it was. Surely they wouldn't have it on milk.

Alice: No, I don't think so because it was on stuff that was imported. Like tires, made of imported rubber.

Augusta: Oh, there were all kinds of things we couldn't get. Since I was teaching, I could manage to get things for the car, but about the food—I don't remember—except there were things we couldn't get, but it was usually something we could do without if we had to.

Alice: That was when you were teaching in Penney Farms, I remember.

Augusta: That's just it. I had a long drive. And I would have a hard time now doing that driving every day. That was about twenty miles one way.

Alice: It was awfully hard, though. You went out there every day, and then you came home, and you were up with Grandma much of the night.

Augusta: Well, really not too much. I mean I'm a person, as you may notice now, who really sleeps when she sleeps. I think I was fortunate enough when I was in the room with Grandma and listening for her. I think I always slept plenty in between times.

Alice: That was still not good for you, though.

Augusta: It wasn't, of course, exactly ideal, but it wasn't that hard on me, and I think I was lucky to get through the whole business as well as I did. And as well as we all did, in general. And then you did so well in school. I remember surprising Gerald. Do you remember when you and I went in to meet him at the bus station in Green Cove around your graduation time?

I remember that you and I had the paper—the *Clay County Crescent*—in which the account of your graduation appeared.

Alice: Oh, yes, I remember how it was. We sent him in to get the paper.

Augusta: Yes, he saw it then. It had your name there as valedictorian, and that was a surprise to him.

Alice: Yes, I remember that.

Augusta: And that was such a nice surprise for us to give to him.

Alice: Well, he was near the top of his class, wasn't he? That was pretty special.

Augusta: He was way up there, and he was the best of the boys. Of course there weren't very many, but still he was the best of the boys.

Alice: There were more boys in his class than there were in mine. I don't know why, because it seems as though by the time I graduated in '49 there would have been fewer boys going into the service.

Augusta: Evidently they hadn't come back to school or something. Now let's see, I wish I could remember everything.

Alice: It's hard to!

Augusta: I can't, unless I can remember something a little unusual, like that "Our Girl."

Alice: Let's see then—I was trying to think of some of the other anecdotes that I remember hearing. Of course one of the things that we thought was so funny was the way that Daddy used to sunbathe in the nude out there at his workshop behind the big oak thicket, and how he shocked the Jehovah's Witnesses when they walked out there unannounced one day when they were making their rounds.

Augusta: We would tell him, you know, "If anyone comes in, at least cover yourself." He said, "Oh, well, they don't have to look if they don't like the appearance of me here in my 'sunsuit.'" And I don't know even if all that sunbathing was so good for him. We hear so much now about too much sun not being good.

Alice: That isn't what got him, of course; he didn't have any cancer or anything like that.

Augusta: No, he had that colon trouble—and of course maybe the sunbathing is good in a way, and in a way it's not. We've heard now not to get too much sun.

Alice: How about his two bad injuries? Can you tell me about them?

Augusta: The one that caused him misery all the rest of his life was the head wound he got in the Philippine Insurrection. He said that he was in a position where he was ambushed by the enemy and would either have to hit the ground where there was a trail of army ants marching along or stand up and be shot. He had to make a quick decision, so he decided to risk the bullets rather than the ants and stood up, and a bullet hit the top of his head. The doctors put a metal plate in there to replace the shattered bone, but it was not right somehow and caused him agonizing headaches for the rest of his life. You may remember that if he exerted himself physically and got overheated, he sometimes passed out.

Alice: Yes, I do.

He told me that when he woke up in the hospital in Manila and saw the white-uniformed nurses all around him, he thought he had died and the nurses were angels. Then, he said, he realized that he *wouldn't* be in heaven, so they *couldn't* be angels.

How about the other one, then? The shoulder injury?

Augusta: The other injury happened when he was in the navy. He and some other men were doing repairs aboard the USS *Leonidas,* when a sledgehammer flew off its handle and hit his right shoulder and did serious injury to it. He was able to overcome that one, though, and it was the other one that caused such pain for him for the rest of his life.

Alice: I remember that he was unable to get disability until 1949, because he hadn't complained enough at the time. Because he had "toughed" it out, they wouldn't believe that the shoulder wound was a disability *(appendix 3)*.

When Daddy had his hernia operation in 1942 so he could go to Pearl Harbor for his job in the civil service, I remember his having to stay in the hospital when he didn't want to. After two days, he wanted out! Also I remember that the doctors scolded him because he made the other men on the ward laugh too much, and they'd all had abdominal surgery, too, so laughing made them hurt.

Augusta: Yes, he didn't like to be told to stay in bed and not move around, and of course he may have hurt himself then, too, by doing more than he should have. Afterward he seemed to have pain, and I think he was feeling miserable once in a while. I often worried then, because he did prefer just to lie down at home, and he certainly didn't want to go back to any hospital. The only thing was to keep him as quiet as possible, and I think really for him it was the best thing that he didn't have to suffer through many more years.

Alice: Yes, rather than be a semi-invalid all that time.

Augusta: That would have been hard on him.

Alice: I remember, though, that he wrote a letter to the Department of the Navy in 1941, right after Pearl Harbor, asking to reenlist. He said in the letter that if they wouldn't let him reenlist, he'd take a war canoe like his ancestors did and go to sea in it to fight the Japanese fleet *(appendix 2)*. Unfortunately, they wouldn't take him because he was too old. But it would have been very hard for him to live long as a semi-invalid or invalid.

Augusta: Yes. And, of course, my mother the same, you know. If she'd had to linger for many years, that would have been hard for her and everybody else.

Alice: Well, actually, she did, didn't she? For the last few years, she was not totally conscious of what was going on.

Augusta: By then, her mind was not good at all—not at all. She wasn't at all the way she had been. It made it hard for her and everybody else. And then you know those illusions she had about people being in the corner. No, she wasn't herself at all. Now that's where Gerald had such a hard time. You remember he had to lift her in and out of cars? He was only fourteen. That was really hard on him. He wasn't even entirely fully grown, but he was strong. Gerald was our "man" at that time.

Alice: Yes, he was. I remember so many things he did.

Augusta: He tended to the car and everything.

Alice: Chopped the wood. Replaced the cylinder rings in the Chevrolet. All kinds of things.

How about you and Daddy, then? How did you get together?

Augusta: Oh, you're going way back!

Alice: Yes, I am.

Augusta: All right. As you know, we came to Florida in 1911 from New Jersey. My father wanted to retire from business and be in a warm climate. And the reason he came to Florida was because of my cousin, Otto Pflug, who wanted to have a nursery down here. If Otto found a good place, Max would come here for his retirement.

Otto came to Jacksonville by water from New York, and happened to meet some Middleburg people who had come in on the *Callie B,* a passenger boat from Middleburg to Jacksonville, and they started talking. They advised him that if he wanted to see any land that he might like to buy, to come on up Black Creek. So he went on with them and came up Black Creek, and they showed him various places, this one among them, that they knew were for sale.

This property was owned by a man named Linstedt. He had built the house we lived in before the time that anyone here knew anything about termites, and that was important insofar as that house would probably have been built differently if people had known about termites. You know, now you're not supposed to have any wood, any lumber, touch the ground. Under the whole house, wherever necessary, there should be blocks—stone or concrete blocks—so that neither the house nor anything leaning on the house touches both the ground and the house, because termites, we are told, will go up any wood, but they won't go up anything else, like concrete. So now they build houses on concrete blocks, if they must have blocks under them. Of course, Linstedt didn't do that, and so the house was full of termites, I suppose, when my parents got it.

Alice: I don't think so, because, according to one story, they didn't even come into the US until about 1924. (*Victor: Earl was told by one of the Baxleys at their lumberyard that termites came to Florida early in the century by way of a shipload of lumber from Mexico to Cedar Point. Alice: It does seem unlikely, though, that there were no native wood-eating termites in Florida before that time.*)

Augusta: The termites didn't come till then?

Alice: Which gave them plenty of time to do their work anyhow. (*Alice: The "old house" had a steadily increasing list to the west because termites were eating the upright logs used for the foundation. Gerald said that a wooden plaque over the door of the dining room that read "Im neuen Heim der alte Segen" ["In the new home the old blessing"] should be translated "In the new home, the old sagging."*)

Augusta: They must have, because at first you wouldn't even notice them if you weren't looking for them. Well, anyhow, after Otto came out here, he liked the place; he liked the looks of it. Of course, he didn't have enough money to buy anything at the time, so he, well, "borrowed"—of course there wasn't really any "borrowing." My father just gave him the six hundred dollars that they wanted for the place.

The house as it looked when Otto Pflug found the property

Now, imagine! Six hundred dollars for thirty acres and a fair-sized house! And then there was a shed out there, which I don't suppose you remember. A good-sized shed and a good-sized house and thirty acres of land for six hundred dollars, just twenty dollars an acre, and you'd probably pay three or four times that now. Now I hear they're selling lots—one acre near Middleburg—and they seem to think they're offering it cheap, at almost one thousand dollars per lot! Imagine! What a difference! So I can't tell you exactly what this place is worth now, but Victor could tell you, and it's a good many thousand.

Alice: When did the Thorps get here, then?

Augusta: The Thorps had read advertisements about Florida back in Kansas. At that time, you know, everyone was invited to come to Florida— that was the big Florida boom. The Thorps wanted to come south where it was warmer, and, of course, Grandpa Thorp was getting older, about my father's age. In 1910, your daddy's father, George Washington Thorp, bought twenty-five acres of land in Russell, just north of the post office. Then, in 1916, he, his wife, Jane, and Earl drove to Florida in their 1914

Model T. The trip took about fifteen days to travel nearly 1200 miles. The roads were under water in some parts of Mississippi. When they arrived, theirs was only the third automobile in Clay County.

In 1917, they traded the Russell property for relinquishment on eighty acres over there to the southwest. I guess you know where it was at Lake Asbury? Really what they had was a lovely place. I don't know if you've been to see that bluff there. I thought it was a lovely place with lovely trees growing on it. Well, anyway, that's the way they happened to come.

Left to right, G. W. Thorp, Max Pflug, Jane Thorp, Marie Pflug, c. 1917

But people in Kansas hated to see Grandpa Thorp leave, because they said at that time, and then afterward again when they asked him to come back, that he was the best repair man or had the best repair institution there. He was the best of any they'd ever had for repairing farm machinery. He and your father after him were such good metal smiths, and your father knew a great deal about metals and about working them, as you know.

Alice: I know he told me all kinds of things about them, which I have forgotten, of course. I always loved to watch when he was working at his forge and hammering and annealing metal things. I liked spending time in his shop, just watching.

Augusta: He made all kinds of nice jewelry out of metals, along with other things.

Well, they came in 1916. The way that his father and my father got together was that we were growing corn here. My father had someone plant it, you know. It was supposed to be for the chickens, and my father always wanted it ground, so he found out that Mr. Thorp out there at Lake Asbury had set up a mill for grinding corn and such.

Alice: He used his mill on that spring, didn't he? They had that nice spring on the place?

Augusta: Well, I don't remember just how it worked. But anyhow, he had the corn ground. He was grinding corn for anyone who would bring it. My father found out about it, so he took corn over, and they got acquainted, and then he invited them over to see us. They came, and they brought your father along, who at that time had just come with them to find out how he liked Florida and to decide whether he wanted to stay here or go back to Kansas. So they brought him along, not any of the rest of the family. His two sisters were already married, and he was the youngest in the family. Your father never did like farm work. I don't know if you knew that or not. He just wasn't interested in things that grow in the ground; at least he didn't want to have anything to do with farming.

Of course, when he was here then, his parents used to come to see us. I'd be home weekends, and that's when we saw each other first. He'd come over here. At that time, my parents would take me down to the train on Sunday afternoons to go back to Spring Glen where I was teaching then, and I guess you heard about their getting home from doing that one day, and Otto was gone. He had just left because he couldn't stand what they were expecting him to do. I can see his part of it because they were expecting—they weren't even paying him—just for his being here, living here, and of course having his board and room and everything, that he should work outside, and he didn't like that kind of work. It wasn't that he didn't like to work; some things he liked to do, but it was just the farm work that he couldn't stand. He didn't want that. He just simply decided that he would leave without telling any of us.

Another reason was, right at that time, his mother had died. She had been living with one of her daughters—she had two married daughters. I think that one may have been in New Mexico. Anyway, she was with one of her daughters, and she had died. Of course, the sisters had sent Otto the notice and when the funeral would be, but when he heard of it, it would already have been over. He wouldn't have had time to get there. Still, he said he would go there anyway and see his sisters, but my father and mother tried to tell him there wasn't much sense in his going. Of course they would have had to pay for the trip. I guess he thought that was heartless of them to say that there wasn't much use in his going. If she had still been alive, or if he could have made it to the funeral, then there would have been some sense to it, but he wouldn't have gotten there until after the funeral, a day or two at the best, and he couldn't do anything for his sisters. They didn't especially want any help from him. So my parents tried to make him understand that a trip like that wouldn't be any good for him. And I don't know if he felt they were heartless or what.

Anyway, he was gone, and that was the last we heard of him. But the worst of it is—or one of the worst parts—that he borrowed money from someone in Middleburg. It was several hundred dollars, according to what Callie Buddington told me. I was shocked when she told me that he had borrowed that and was going to send it right back to them. Of course, they probably thought that we were here, and if they loaned him money, we'd see to it that they got it right back. I don't know what she thought, but anyway, whoever it was—I think it was Callie Buddington—she gave him the money, and they never heard from him again. They always wanted us to tell them his address, and we didn't even know that. I don't know if they believed that—that we didn't know—or what. I know it was kind of a bad situation.

Alice: How did Daddy work into this then?

Augusta: Your dad—I've gotten a little bit too far into the past, insofar as your dad was concerned. You know that was right at the beginning of the war—the First World War—and they wanted all the young men to enlist. They weren't drafting anyone at first, but young men were expected to enlist.

Alice: I thought you were saying that because Otto had left, probably about 1914 or 1915, they got Daddy to do some things around here.

Augusta: No, that wasn't then—that was later. I was thinking of the earlier time when Raymond Hendricks was working here. I don't think that your dad and Otto even knew each other. He and I got acquainted after Otto had left.

And then we got to the war, and they were, naturally, glad to have volunteers, aside from having to draft men of a certain age, and your father at that time still would have been in that draft age, but he volunteered. He wasn't drafted into the army. He volunteered, and this must have been after we had known the Thorps for a year or so.

One Sunday afternoon in the spring of 1918, when my parents had taken me to the train, your dad was on the train, too. He knew that I was going in on Sundays. So we were together on the train, and when we got to Jacksonville, I could go out to where I was boarding in South Jacksonville at any time, and his train for wherever he was going wasn't leaving for a while, so we spent some time in Jacksonville together. I remember we walked from the depot up to Hemming Park. You know, Hemming Park was always a pretty place. Anyway, we spent the evening in Jacksonville together. My train out to Spring Glen didn't go till about seven o'clock. It wasn't far to go, but I did have to go back to the depot. And then that's when we said good-bye to each other because he said that he was enlisting, and they had ordered him to report on a certain day. We promised to write to each other. Then, of course, the war lasted from 1914 to 1918. It ended on the eleventh day of the eleventh month at eleven o'clock.

During that time, there was another unusually funny thing. I guess you've heard me talk about Harry Wimberly, one of the twins who wanted to learn Latin and algebra in Highland where I started teaching? They couldn't afford to go to high school, and Mr. Beggs, the superintendent, asked if I could teach Latin and algebra at the Highland school. I could, so I was hired.

Anyway, I was writing to your father *and* Harry, who had both asked me to write. Harry used to come here to see us because he had been one of my best pupils when I was first teaching. He, too, then went into the navy. I've been talking about army, but they both were in the *navy*. So I was writing to both of them in the *navy*.

One time I had two postal cards that I had written to the two of them, and I mailed the postal cards at the same time. I did notice that their addresses—you know we were never given their exact addresses—were a general navy address. I noticed theirs were the same, but I didn't think much of that because I thought that all the navy people got their mail through that address. So I mailed them, but somehow they stuck together, and it was—let me get this right now, who was which. It was Harry who got the two cards stuck together, and he noticed the name R. E. Thorp, and he noticed, since they were postal cards, that they each had my name on the outside, too. He could see that I had written both and they had stuck together. It was Harry's that must have been on top, and he got that, and then the other one was underneath to R. E. Thorp. He knew that they must be on the same ship because of some number or something on there, and he looked around for him and found him.

They thought that was very funny, and I thought it was funny when I heard about it. Anyway, that's the way they got acquainted. They got to be friends because they were on the ship together for a while. Then, when everybody came home from the war, by that time the Thorps had moved back to Kansas. George and Jane didn't like it here anyway after your father left because they were there alone—those two old folks, or elderly folks then. So they sold that place, and other people have lived there since. I don't know if you even know where they were.

Alice: Yes, I know where they were.

Augusta: Anyway, then, after the war was over, your father didn't come right home because he stayed there for the Marshall Plan—you know, they had volunteers to stay there. The US was helping France after the war because of what the Germans had done there, and the US was sending food there because food was scarce.

Earl at the Eiffel Tower, France, c. 1919

Alice: Didn't we decide that was the Hoover deal? The Marshall Plan was the Second World War? *(Alice: It was Hoover's American Relief Administration.)*

Augusta: We may have talked about it, if you can remember that.

Alice: Hoover went over there himself, I know, and he was grief-stricken, seeing the poverty and the starving children.

Augusta: All I know is instead of coming right home as most of them did, your father stayed over there to help with whatever the Americans were doing. They volunteered to stay there and help, and I'm sure they were paid for that. Then, when he finally decided to come on home, he was going to go straight on to Kansas, where his folks were. And in the meantime, he had had another letter from me, and—let's see—when did my father die? In 1919. So he must—no, my father was dead by the time that your father was ready to come back, because the war ended in 1918, and then this Hoover Plan, or whatever it was—the US helping France—was going on. Then your father came home. It must have been 1919. And then, instead of going right on to Kansas, where his folks were, he stopped here in Florida and came to see us—maybe putting "me" for "us." Anyway, he came here, and I think it was right about then that we decided to get married.

Alice: Didn't you tell me one time about Harry Wimberly's saying something to Daddy like, "You got to her first"? He said he was intending to propose to you?

Augusta: Oh, yes, Harry Wimberly. You know that was ridiculous. I always tried not to have my older students get infatuated, and I know that I discouraged Harry all the time. I would always say, "Harry, I'm five years older than you are. Now you must listen to what I say and do so and so." I'd tell him about the nice girls that I knew who would be glad to have him ask them out. I wasn't going to go out with a student five years younger than I.

Now, how old was he? Well, five years younger, anyhow. Probably about sixteen or seventeen, and you know that's quite a difference at that age.

But Harry and your father were good friends by that time. They got together in the navy that way, and they thought that was so funny, and we all did, about those cards sticking together and introducing them when they'd been on the same ship together and not known each other. That really was a strange incident.

And then, you see, we were married in—oh, then your grandparents again. You know, after your father was gone—I mean from Florida and in the navy—his parents had gone back to Kansas, and they had sold that place out here. But anyway, I just wanted you to know that those cards brought those two together, and Harry used to come to see us a lot after we were married.

Alice: I think you have pictures of Daddy and Harry in the den.

Augusta: And, let's see, when did I finally lose track of Harry? He may have gone somewhere else, another part of the country. Now for years I don't know anything about the Wimberlys. Harry had a twin brother that died before this time of which I'm speaking, and since then I heard his one younger brother had died. And then there was a little Wimberly girl whom they nicknamed Boots. I can't remember all those names. In the course of time, when you don't see people at all, they kind of seem to drop out of mind.

But anyway, when your father and I decided we would get married, I was teaching in Ortega, and there was an end-of-the-year school picnic scheduled for June 19. I skipped the picnic to get married. My mother and Auntie were here, and they came and were our witnesses.

Earl and Augusta after their wedding, 1920

At that time, Auntie was teaching at Virginia Intermont. This was in June, and she was going to go back to teach swimming there that summer, and she was going to take my mother along because she thought it would be cooler there than in hot Florida. So my mother agreed to go up there with her. We hadn't told Raymond Hendricks *(Alice: Raymond Hendricks was resident caretaker for several years.),* who was here in the little house with his family. It's gone now. You know where that was? We hadn't told them anything about my mother and sister leaving or the two of us being here, so they were really surprised. After my mother and my sister had been our witnesses at the wedding ceremony in Jacksonville—we didn't go into any church, it was a civil ceremony—they left to go up to Virginia, and then your father and I came out here, and Raymond Hendricks was really surprised that my mother wasn't back, nor my sister, and especially when we told them that we were married.

Of course Raymond never said anything, but I know that what he missed so much after that was the Model T that had been practically his for the using. I'm sure that when we weren't here and the car was here, which often happened, they used it, which was perfectly all right. He was our driver at the time and also took care of things on the property. My father never would touch the car. He never would drive. He bought the car, and that was all. It was really my father's car, but it was Raymond who was the driver and who took care of it to see that it was always in running order. So I can see that he missed it when your father took over after we were married. That was our car then. I can see that wasn't so nice for Raymond. We didn't need Raymond then, because at that time your father was always repairing cars here. People would bring him cars, and he would make what little money he could make that way.

Of course we were in Jacksonville a while, too, and I worked in an office there, and he worked with welding. So you see there were all kinds of things happening in those days until we finally got settled out here. After that, I taught only in those schools that were within reach, like Doctors Inlet, or Penney Farms, or Orange Park, so that I could be home at least in the evenings and on the weekends, and I guess you know about things since then.

Alice: Some of them, yes.

Augusta: My first baby was prematurely born, and I can see now that I did too much. I taught in Middleburg part of the time when I was pregnant, and the class that I was teaching was upstairs. It was much like Doctors Inlet—a big building, and upstairs were the rooms for the upper grades. So every day from the schoolyard I had to make this high climb up and down those stairs several times. I know, now that I know more about these things, doing that was not good. Climbing stairs is one of the things a pregnant woman is really not supposed to do much of. It strains her. I think that's probably what I did to mess myself up.

Alice: It's hard to say, of course.

Augusta: And it may all be for the best. Anyway I'm thankful to have the rest of you. There was never any trouble there. But I think I was also more careful.

Let's see now. After that, I taught at those various schools of which you know, and it was mostly those places I remember—Middleburg, Penney Farms, Doctors Inlet. I think it was just those three after I was married.

Alice: Orange Park?

Augusta: Oh, yes—I was in Orange Park. Yes, four schools. I always took off a whole term or nearly a whole term in between times. I wouldn't start a term if I knew I couldn't finish it or didn't want to finish it, and in those days teachers didn't do as they do nowadays—teach until the last minute before the baby is born. I don't think that's a good idea, not only because of other reasons but also because of the mother, herself. In the classroom, I stood up most of the day. I wasn't one of these teachers to sit down and stay there at the desk. I would go back and forth in the room and see that everyone was busy doing what he or she should be doing.

Alice: Which is a very wise thing to do.

Augusta: Yes. I imagine that *you* don't just sit down in the classroom, although you don't have children in class.

Alice: No, I don't.

Well, if you're not worn out yet, I wanted to ask you about the animals.

Augusta: Animals! Well—animals—I don't—if you want to know about dogs, ask Victor. Our family had a bulldog in New Jersey that used to frighten visitors by peering around the basement door at them. And here, we have always had that pet cemetery out under the pecan tree near the garage. That's where we buried our dogs and cats. We marked each grave with a seashell or a pretty rock of some sort. We've had lots of pets.

Alice: No, I mean before Victor's time. You had a horse, and you had that sheep that was strange, didn't you?

Augusta: The only thing about that ram, named Snooky, was that Auntie declared the sheep wouldn't bother anyone, and then he butted her down. She couldn't very well say we hadn't warned her that sheep can be dangerous, but she didn't believe that.

Alice: Did the horse have a name?

Augusta. Goodness, we had several horses.

Alice. Oh, I didn't know that. I thought there was just one.

How about that pig that you told me about that wandered in?

Augusta: I remember about the pig. We called him Gruntsie. The horses and mules we had must not have impressed me much, but I can tell you about that little hog.

One night we were just having supper, and we heard something kind of squawk outside. I think it must have been warm weather, and everything was open. There was kind of a "squeak-squeak" out there. And when we looked, there was the cutest little hog; it couldn't have been more than a few weeks old. It was just standing out there squawking, so we went out, and it wasn't timid. It just let us come right up and pet it, and then we got something to eat for him or her—I've forgotten its gender—and after we fed it, it followed us around. I guess it was expecting we would have more food. It stayed right there. We didn't do anything to put it into any enclosure; it stayed right by the house.

And naturally it grew, and after a while, it got really quite large, and we were afraid it might eat something it shouldn't or bite off something it shouldn't, so we put it into a pen, and then some of the people around here were saying, "That'll make you a good roast." Well, we didn't want any of that. It was such a pet, almost like part of the family, that we didn't want that. Finally, though, it had gotten so strong it would try to play with us and almost knock us down—not viciously, just a little rough. So now let me see if I can remember to whom we gave it. I think either we didn't know or didn't want to know to whom my parents gave it.

Alice: Whoever that was probably *did* have a nice roast!

Augusta: Because that's what they'd been telling us. "It will make a grand roast. Just a good size, young, and would be so tender—a lovely roast." Well, that would make us sick because we raised it from a baby. Well, that's the only thing I can tell you about that pig. There may be somebody around yet who remembers that and could tell you what really happened to it, but I might not even want to know.

Alice: How about Maushie the cat? That was when you and Daddy were just married, wasn't it?

Augusta: I know it was a big pet, but I don't remember anything special about Maushie. I do remember Elmer, though, the black and white cat that won over your father in the 1940s. He had never cared much for cats until Elmer decided that Earl was "his person." After that, they were nearly inseparable. Do you remember that Elmer would go to bed with your daddy, and then when Earl was asleep, Elmer would come to us to let him out for the night?

Alice: Oh, yes. Elmer was a special cat. He went wandering but always came back. And he always announced his return with loud meows from the edge of the yard.

Earl's favorite cat, Elmer

Would you please tell me more about how you traveled from here to Green Cove Springs and Jacksonville?

Augusta: When we first moved here, there was no bridge across Black Creek between Middleburg and the mouth of the Creek, which was about sixteen miles. At both places—Middleburg and the mouth of the Creek and halfway in between—in three places, there were ferries. Then car travel started. First it was just all horse and mule travel. Anyway, the animals that were new to the ferry were usually afraid at first, but they soon got used to it, if they did it maybe daily or often. I know that we did have some horses. We had several, and one or two of them were afraid of the water. And also since then, three bridges have been built to replace the ferries. And, you know, you cross one of them often down here.

Marguerite with magnolias at the railroad bridge

Alice: And one in Middleburg?

Augusta: One in Middleburg and one at the mouth of the Creek.

Alice: The big one up on Highway 17?

Augusta: Yes, and then, of course, there's the railroad bridge, the Atlantic Coastline Railroad Bridge that I didn't count with those other bridges. The Atlantic Coastline—you know, where the train stopped, and I could get on to return to Spring Glen. Then the ferryman's salary was, let's see, it must have been less than forty dollars a month.

Alice: He and his family had their place to live provided, didn't they?

Augusta: Yes, of course they had that ferry house.

Alice: And did they always have to lower the cable at night?

Augusta: Yes, the cable was lowered to keep boats and boaters from hitting it in the dark. It had to be down, also, day or night, for the passenger boats that ran from Middleburg to Jacksonville and back. It was too low for them to pass under.

Alice: At sundown, I guess it was?

Augusta: It was actually a little later in winter. But it was down during the night.

Alice: I remember that if we had something to go to, we had to make sure we told the ferryman to leave the cable up, and then we'd put ourselves across and let it down.

Augusta: We often had to put ourselves across, and also sometimes we just had to come way around. That's only we; other people may not have had to go as far as we did to go around. But if we came to the ferry and the cable was down, we'd have to go back by Rideout and come around that way on Highway 17 or come across the Middleburg Bridge, which of course would be quite a way out of the ordinary distance. One other choice would have been to leave the car over on the other side. Usually they had a boat over there so people could put themselves across who maybe wanted to come back and pull the ferry across themselves. Pull up the cable and all that. That cable was very heavy to raise.

Alice: Yes, I remember doing that.

Augusta: But anyway, it was a mess always with that ferry, sometimes with hyacinths, and then sometimes the cable was broken.

Augusta trapped in a hyacinth blockade just beginning its bloom

Alice: Yes, I'd forgotten about the hyacinths. Sometimes we couldn't even get out on the Creek. And I remember that sometimes they were so thick we couldn't even swim. As beautiful as they were when they bloomed, they were really a menace. When there were a lot of hyacinths, but we could still swim between them, you used to beat the floating islands of hyacinths with an oar or a stick to scare away any alligators or snakes that might be in them.

Augusta: You might mention that sometimes the Creek was *completely* covered with hyacinths. That made boating or moving the ferry difficult.

Alice: Who was the first ferryman that you remember over there?

Augusta: I don't even remember their names. There weren't very many. For a long time it was Falana. (*Victor: Falana's wife tragically died of "the miseries," according to Falana. Earl, Augusta, and Victor went to visit her shortly before she died.*)

Alice: And there were several Adamses, weren't there, or at least one or two?

Augusta: Yes, Falana and Adams are two names that I can remember.

Alice: Raymond Frisbee.

Augusta: You remember him?

Alice: Yes, I do. And then there was Tirl Phillips.

Augusta: Well, put Frisbee and Phillips then, because they certainly were there, too.

Alice: Oh, yes, there was Uncle—Uncle Petty. Uncle what's-his-name Petty—that relative, I think, of the Powells? *Sam* Petty. A portly fellow. He ran it for a while. *(Victor: Also add Thomas and Joe Starling and Burtis Boree as ferrymen.)*

Augusta: I don't remember him. Anyway, they always found someone who would do it for at least a while, but you might say that automobiles were just beginning to appear at that time when—who's the one I told you always walked for his check?

Alice: Oh, yes—Adams?

Augusta: Falana?

Alice: Falana? I don't remember now.

Augusta: I think it was Falana. Falana walked to Green Cove Springs, which is a walk of more than ten miles from the ferry, for his monthly paycheck. He didn't want to accept the offer of people who would take him in a car because he was afraid of automobiles.

Alice: Dangerous things.

Augusta: Yes, he wasn't going to ride in "one of them things." Could you imagine somebody walking in this kind of hot summer weather, for instance, and of course in the cold in winter, which wasn't too pleasant, either? But imagine walking more than ten miles each way to get a little check like that, which of course seemed to him like a big check, but that's all he had.

Alice: I guess so.

Augusta: Well, it would certainly be hard to have anyone do that today—I mean be *willing* to do that. And besides that, he was not a young man. It wasn't as though he should have been doing a lot of walking.

Alice: Do you know how he spelled his name—Falana?

Augusta: F-a-l-a-n-a. Fa-la-na.

Well now, so much for the ferry, I guess.

Alice: No, because I remember that Daddy rebuilt something on the ferry one time, didn't he? I remember his pulling me in a little wagon on the sand road to go over there, and I stayed with him while he worked on it. I must have been about four years old.

Augusta: He may have worked on it. I don't know the kind of work he did on it, though.

Alice: I think he did a great deal of work on the aprons.

Augusta: Well, he may have done so, if you remember that. (*Victor: The aprons, the adjustable, hinged tracks that made it possible to get onto the ferry at all levels of the tide, needed to be made longer because cars were being built lower and were scraping on the shorter aprons as they drove on and off the ferry.*)

Augusta's car on the ferry at the Rideout Crossing

Alice: The boys were in school with you, and he was taking care of me, so he pulled me over there to the ferry in Victor's wagon.

Augusta: Well, you see, I probably didn't even know much about what he was doing there, because I guess I was gone before he got started and then came back after he was already through. You know I used to come back from school rather late sometimes.

Alice: Yes.

Augusta: So I really don't know about that. You'll have to write what you can remember.

Alice: Another thing about the ferry—I remember it had to be pulled up on the bank when the water got too high.

Augusta: Well, when the Creek was covered with hyacinths or there was a flood, the ferry couldn't be used.

The Billow

Alice: I can remember their pulling it all the way out and up the bank to keep it from being washed away.

Augusta: Oh, yes, there were times when you couldn't get to it because there was too much water and the ferry couldn't be pulled.

Alice: And then it was always an exciting thing to get up the clay hill that went up from the ferry, too, when it was rainy. It was also exciting to go down it.

Augusta: Oh, that hill was awful. People just can't even imagine those things now.

Alice: I guess almost without exception the men that ran the ferry were interesting characters.

Augusta: Well, they were, more or less, because not everyone would be likely to want a job in which practically day or night there could be people who came there and didn't know how to get across without the ferry. There was always a boat left there, too, on the far side, so that you could go over and get the ferry yourself. But you know, people who were not used to that or maybe were complete strangers around here wouldn't know what to do.

Alice: And there were those people, too, who, when the ferry was on this side, came to the other side and thought they could drive across. I remember there were several instances of that, too.

Augusta: There were all kinds of such instances.

Alice: Those people sank.

Augusta: I don't remember anyone being drowned there, though.

Alice: No, I don't think any of them were drowned.

Augusta: But there were instances of cars going overboard or horses going into the water. I do know that, but I don't think anyone ever was seriously hurt or killed.

Alice: Wasn't it Raymond Frisbee that motorized the ferry? Wasn't he the one that secured a boat on the side of the ferry and let the outboard motor push it across?

Augusta: I don't know.

Alice: Or was that Tirl? I don't remember now. Gerald will remember that.

Augusta: He may remember. That didn't make too much of an impression on me either. I do remember the boat, though.

Alice: Because that was the height of luxurious travel! You didn't have to pull yourself across on the cable anymore.

Augusta: Yes, and it was easier on the ferryman, but of course gas was cheaper then. I guess now they wouldn't even think of doing that because it would take a lot of gasoline. But in those days, I guess nobody worried much about gasoline because it was so inexpensive. It was, I think, about fourteen cents or less a gallon.

Alice: We'll leave the ferry for a few minutes. Victor was saying yesterday that he thought it would be very interesting if you would tell about the way you used to get to Jacksonville and to Green Cove Springs—the way you had to make the trips when you first got here.

Augusta: People along the Creek from Middleburg eastward toward the Saint Johns River would usually make weekly trips to Jacksonville on the *Callie B* or one of the other passenger boats from Middleburg to Jacksonville—a five-hour trip. Imagine!

Alice: Five hours! Now we make it in about forty-five minutes in the car, and that's when the traffic is bad.

Augusta: It was a whole day to go in, and then you'd have a few hours in there.

Alice: About how early in the morning would you have to catch the *Callie B*?

The Callie B

Augusta: You see, they left Middleburg at six in the morning and would be here at seven. We'd be down at the dock at seven o'clock. If we had the flag stuck out on our dock, it meant "Please stop," and they would pick up whatever passengers wanted to go. We used a flag in daylight and a lantern in the dark to signal the boat.

In summer, when I had no school, I was the one that got the groceries. I'd get to Jacksonville downtown where the boats are—I guess you know that part of town. There were none of the big markets then, but there was a grocery store, whose name I have forgotten, on Bay Street near where the boats landed. I could get the groceries there, and they would be shipped down to the boat. Fortunately, I didn't have to carry several big bags of groceries. They would send them down, and the boat would leave at two in the afternoon to return.

Alice: That didn't leave you much time there at all, then.

Augusta: It was all right. We'd leave here at seven o'clock and get there somewhere around nine thirty or something. No—wait.

Alice: No, it couldn't be. If it left Middleburg at six o'clock, was it a five-hour trip from there or from here?

Augusta: It was a four-hour trip from here.

Alice: So it was eleven o'clock when you got there.

Augusta: We got there at eleven o'clock, and then when I went, I'd go straight up to the grocery store and get the groceries, and after I paid, they would send them down to the boat, which left at two o'clock. That's the way it was.

Alice: And got back here about six o'clock?

Augusta: We would get back home at about six o'clock. And then there were always my father and mother down there at the dock, or whoever was here. We'd get the groceries off and everything else that I had.

In Jacksonville, after I had gotten the groceries, I could go, or whoever was with me could go, and get the other things from other stores. But of course if we went to other stores, we couldn't have many other things. I guess we could have had other things sent down to the boat, but we didn't. We carried what we could carry, but with the groceries, that was just too much to try to take much more.

Alice: Do you remember what it cost to ride in there and back again?

Augusta: Yes, it was fifty cents one way.

Alice: Isn't that something! Do you remember another boat besides the *Callie B*? Was it the *Callie B* that sank up there at Devil's Elbow?

Augusta: No, the other passenger boat was that boat that Auntie and I were on. That was the *Billow*. But that was later, probably about 1914 or 1915.

Alice: Oh, yes—the *Billow*. I remember that name.

Augusta: But that was later, and the *Billow* was a much bigger boat than the *Callie B*. The *Billow* had an upstairs, an upper deck.

Alice: They were both tugboats? Or were they classed as that?

Augusta: Oh, no, no. They weren't tugboats. They were regular passenger boats. Both of them. And the *Billow* even had that upper deck. I think that's what made it top-heavy and why it tipped over. You heard about my sister and me being on it when it tipped over, didn't you?

Alice: No! I don't remember that. I knew that it turned over, but I didn't know you and Auntie were on it.

Augusta: Yes, we had been in New York that summer. She and I went to New York to Columbia University to take courses. She was the one who wanted to go, and I felt it would do me good to take some courses and get some more college credits.

We went up there together, and a friend of Auntie's went with us. I don't remember her name. Anyway, this friend of Auntie's, and Auntie, and I were up there at Columbia University in New York for six weeks in summer. We went up and also came back by boat. There were big boats going from Jacksonville to New York, and we liked that very much. We liked it up there. We had a room together—the three of us—that we rented, and this friend paid her share of it.

We took turns fixing lunches. The one who was fixing lunches would also buy what was needed for lunch—bread and such. Something like you and I eat now for lunch. And then we'd get together there at noon and eat our lunches. Sometimes we'd come in one at a time when we were delayed somewhere, but when each of us would come in, we'd eat our lunch and then meet again in the late afternoon.

That was during the time when there were a lot of nice peaches ripening and other fruits and berries. Anyway, my mother was here, and she put up *(Alice: "Put up" meant "preserved.")* all kinds of fruit, and I remember that she sent us some jars of strawberry jam and some peach jam, and they were just *so* good. Fortunately it all arrived in good condition. But we were thinking of her here in the very hot kitchen right in the middle of summer putting up preserves for us and then going to the trouble of packing them really carefully. It all arrived in good condition, and we enjoyed it.

We had quite an interesting summer there, but I don't know if I ever did get much credit for all I did up there. I can't even remember now just what courses I took.

Anyway, it was interesting, and since I could be with the girls, I wasn't at all lonesome. I did still at the time have friends there, too, because

Newark isn't far from there, where my friends were when we had lived there. I even visited them on weekends during those six weeks in New York. I, alone, because my sister and this other girl didn't know the people I visited.

You may have heard me speak of my boss at *Schirmer's*, where I had worked a little bit in the office in that music business before we came to Florida. The reason I got that job so easily was that I knew German. You know, many of the songs came in and even letters in German, and Schirmer is a German name—you know, a *schirm* is an umbrella. Anyway, I went and visited with the Schirmers as well as other friends. When they found out I was in New York, they invited me. So on weekends, sometimes, Auntie and her friend would go somewhere, and I'd go and visit some of my old friends. Auntie had some friends, too, but of course I was older and had been ahead of her in school there and so had more friends *(appendix 9)*.

Augusta and Marguerite at Columbia University, c. 1915, where they took summer classes

Augusta's granddaughters and Marguerite's nieces, Terry Fortner (left) and Suzy Thorp (right), visit Columbia University in 2011, almost one hundred years after Augusta and Marguerite attended summer classes

Anyway, it was an interesting summer. When we came back, though, things got a little *too* interesting. We came to Jacksonville on the boat. We came back on a Friday, and that was the day that the *Callie B* and the *Billow* were both in Jacksonville. We could have gotten on the *Billow*— no—what I should have said is we *could* have gotten on the *Callie B*, but we liked the *Billow* because it had that upper deck. We got on the *Billow*. I know it was the *Billow* that tipped over! And when we got out of Jacksonville a little way that afternoon, a really hard wind came up—a thunderstorm and a wind—and the boat was a little top-heavy anyway with its upper deck, and it just turned over.

Alice: Oh! In the Saint Johns River, not on Black Creek?

Augusta: Yes, in the river before we got to Black Creek, but still near Jacksonville fortunately, and fortunately not too far from the riverbank. I held on to my pocketbook for a while, and then I stopped holding on to it. I had all the money that we had left, and I dropped my pocketbook, fortunately, right on the boat. I got it back later when they pulled the boat up and found it, and of course, my name was in there somewhere, so they knew whose it was. *(Alice: A "pocketbook" was a purse.)*

Anyway, I got it back and in there—did I ever show you that pin that I gave to Auntie? Where is it now? Who has it now?

Alice: That garnet pin?

Augusta: Yes, that one that I said was a valuable brooch.

Alice: I think that's the one that was stolen, wasn't it?

Augusta: Oh, I guess that's it—yes. I knew I didn't have it anymore. I think I gave it to Auntie, and then it was stolen from her cabin in Virginia.

Anyway, the boat tipped over. And first thing we knew, we were in the water, and I know they laughed about me because I had a hat on. I guess Auntie's hat came off, and she lost it, because we were all wearing hats then. But anyway, I still had my hat on. And fortunately for us, there were two Chalker boys on the boat—you've heard of Chalker, the name, I guess, in Middleburg—and they were about our age, in their late teens or early twenties. Anyway, they had been on a canoe trip, and they had a canoe with them. And so the two Chalker boys and my sister and I hung on to the canoe, which had fallen off the deck into the river with us. My pocketbook was gone. I didn't know just where it was.

Alice: Where was your friend?

Augusta: Well, she didn't live in Florida

Alice: Oh, she wasn't with you then.

Augusta: That was someone my sister had gotten acquainted with in Virginia.

Anyway, it was just my sister and I and the two Chalker boys, and we were hanging on to the canoe and pushed ourselves ashore because we weren't very far from there. And then we went to a house where they had a telephone.

It was lucky for us that we were with the Chalker boys because the Chalkers had a store in Middleburg, and so the boys telephoned and told their parents what had happened and asked if they would meet us at Peoria. That's where the night train stopped.

There was an eleven o'clock train—I think there still is—that comes out from Jacksonville, going south. It's the Atlantic Coast Line, and I don't know if it stops at those little places now, but at that time, that late-night train would get to Peoria about eleven o'clock. So those boys asked their parents to meet us there, to come from Middleburg, meet us at Peoria, take us home, and then go on to Middleburg.

Alice: Meanwhile, you were all sopping wet?

Augusta: We were sopping wet, but it was hot weather, so we didn't mind it, but I know we looked bedraggled. I know we looked a sight, and of course I don't know if the others still had their hats, but I know that *I* had *my* hat. You know how a straw hat would hang bedraggled. I must have looked beautiful! Oh, and I had torn my sleeve. I had one sleeve all ripped open. We must have looked a sight when we got on the train. Well then, neither my sister nor I had much money. She didn't have much with her, and I had lost my pocketbook. I got it back later, which was very fortunate because it also had that valuable brooch in it. I know we were just so lucky the whole way through.

Then the four of us went and had some supper down at the railroad station, and then, of course, we had to wait until it was time for the train to go. And I think we just waited. The train left some time around ten o'clock. I really don't know whether we took a walk in between times or sat right there in the railroad station. Anyway, they stayed, and we stayed right together. And then they bought tickets for us, which, of course, we repaid later. But we couldn't even have bought tickets on the train and couldn't have let our parents know because they had no phone.

Well, then, when we finally got on the train, dripping, I suppose, still pretty wet even at that late hour, I guess the people were wondering what in the world was the matter with us. Anyway, we got to Peoria, and at Peoria, sure enough, there were the Chalkers, Mr. and Mrs. Chalker.

They had a buggy with enough room for all of us in it, and do you know that they took us home here first? They didn't go straight on to Middleburg and expect somebody to call for us there. They came here, which was a bad road at the time. But they brought us home, and I know that my father and mother had been worried because they'd been down there at the dock waiting for the boat to come. And of course the *Billow* didn't even come. But the *Callie B* came by, so they thought the *Billow* would come, too. They were expecting us on the *Billow* because they knew we liked it. And when the other boat went by, it didn't stop because there was nobody on it to ask it to stop. But they thought that because that other boat had come, the *Billow* would come soon.

Alice: Had the *Callie B* left earlier so your parents didn't even know what had happened?

Augusta: They didn't know what had happened. They didn't know anything had happened. They were just waiting for the *Billow* to come.

Alice: No, I mean the people on the *Callie B* might have known. It seems like they could have stopped to let your parents know.

Augusta: But the people on the *Callie B* didn't know we were on the *Billow*.

Alice: Ohhhhh, of course!

Augusta: See, they wouldn't know there was anybody here expecting somebody, because it was dark, and my parents would have had the light on at the dock if they had expected any boat to stop then, when they'd seen the *Billow* coming around the bend at Little Black Creek.

Well, anyway, we got here then, thanks to the Chalkers, and we felt very much indebted to them, but in later years we didn't even keep up the friendship. Neither my sister nor I was the kind of girl that went after boys. We weren't, and you know although they made various offers, hints, you know, about coming to see us—the kind of girls we were, we didn't even take any advantage of that when we should have been only grateful to them and invited them and maybe had them to dinner or something. We never even thought of anything like that.

Alice: You had been discouraged by your father anyhow, hadn't you? I remember you told me he was so disappointed that you and Auntie were girls, because he wanted sons. And you said he never got over that disappointment. Didn't he even have your hair cut like a boy's hair when you were little?

Augusta: Yes. And he certainly didn't want us to get married, because he considered the life of a married woman to be difficult, confining, and restrictive. He encouraged us to become educated and have careers. That was one of his philosophies. And remember that this was the time when not many women had careers or even college educations.

Alice: What were some of his other philosophies?

Augusta: Oh, there were many. To give you just a couple, he also said that many people say they would like to live their lives over, but one life is enough for anyone. And when he chose his burial plot in what now is Oakland Cemetery, he chose a spot under a big oak tree, because he said that becoming part of a great tree provided a person a kind of immortality.

Alice: I would have to agree with all of those philosophies but not with his attitude about you and Auntie not being boys!

But then what happened? Weren't there other people on the boat besides you and the Chalker boys?

Augusta: There were very few passengers. There was really, I think, only one other man who had intended to come out this way. And I can see him now as plainly as I can see you.

Alice: But nobody was hurt?

Augusta: Nobody was hurt. Nobody was hurt or certainly not drowned. No, it was fortunate that there were not many people on the boat. And it was fortunate that the boat was where it was when it turned over. It had gone far enough in toward shore so that it had struck bottom and had drifted in that way. I don't think we could have waded ashore. It was too deep for that, but then you know we had the canoe to hang on to.

Of course my parents had just given us up. They thought something must have happened so that the boat couldn't even leave Jacksonville. They didn't know what had happened. Of course they were very glad when we did arrive and we were all right. But we didn't have anything. We had left our suitcases on board, and we knew that they would be sopping wet if they were ever gotten out, which they were, naturally. Well, that was that episode. I thought you'd heard about that.

Alice: I guess I had, but I'd never heard the full details.

Augusta: I know my sister and I always had to think of that. We often spoke of it. That was the biggest adventure we had together. It was a kind of a climax to our visit in New York.

But then another nice thing that happened was that only a very few days later, a boat stopped at our dock, and somebody came up here with our suitcases and even with my handbag.

Alice: That is remarkable, isn't it?

Augusta: And there wasn't a thing missing! There was some money, not a great deal, but certainly a number of dollars. Possibly something like twenty or twenty-five dollars. I think I had about that much left. Anyway, there wasn't much money, and my sister didn't have any money with her because she always wanted me to carry hers, too. We put ours all together. And then when our suitcases came, of course we were glad of that, but everything was sopping wet. And we had brought back a number of books that we had bought that summer, and they were ruined.

Alice: What a shame!

Augusta: And there were all kinds of other things that should not have gotten wet. And our clothes, of course, had all gotten wet. My sister had a very pretty, dark blue, velvet dress that was hot for here in summer, but up in New York it was all right. Even in warm weather it wasn't usually that hot up there. And you know how wet velvet would look. Her dress was just ruined. It's too bad because she liked that dress so well. Otherwise, we were all right, and that was the main thing.

Alice: I guess they revived the *Billow* and had it going again soon?

Augusta: Oh, yes, and then they changed it a little bit to make it less top-heavy. They had been working on it before anything happened because they wanted more seats up on the top deck, and they had just gotten it too top-heavy. And then, if it hadn't been for that storm we had, nothing would have happened, anyway. But it was one of those awfully strong gusts that knocked it over. Well now, so much for that.

Alice: Then which one was it that sank up here at Devil's Elbow?

Augusta: Oh, that was what reminded me of the *Billow* adventure. That was—

Alice: It was Captain Larson. I know that.

Augusta: Yes, it was Captain Larson who ran a boat regularly, but it wasn't the *Callie B,* and it wasn't the *Della C*, both of which came regularly. But Larson—

Alice: I probably know the name and just can't think of it now.

Alice Marie Thorp Duxbury

Augusta: Yes. I should know it.

Alice: I'm sure Victor will remember, but I just don't. *(Victor: It was the* Alert.*)*

Augusta: Anyway, what happened with him, what people thought—although they couldn't exactly accuse him of it because nobody was sure—was that he might have been drinking too much, because he knew the Creek so well. He'd been on it day and night, dark and daylight. He knew the Creek, and he knew Devil's Elbow up there where the cemetery is. He shouldn't have capsized.

It was right up there at what is called Devil's Elbow where he ran too close to shore. He made too quick a turn, I think, which no one would have expected him to do. And that night there wasn't any storm—at that time, anyway. He made that turn, the boat turned over, and he fell in.

He had two or three passengers—men—who had been doing some business in Jacksonville, and he always had quite some money on board because people would stop him when he went in, in the morning. They'd give him orders like getting some sacks of fertilizer or something like that. We'd had him bring out stuff like that—food for the animals or sacks of fertilizer that we couldn't very well get anywhere else and just carry. And it was supposed that on that night on the boat, when they finally got the boat up they didn't—let's see—he drowned? Had you heard that?

Alice: I think so.

Augusta: They found him. They got to the boat right away, as soon as they could, but the thing is they did not find any money. Now of course, it's possible—you know, he had a regular cabin and a drawer or something where he kept his things in a desk, but he was always right there by it. But of course when it tipped over—nobody to this day knows—well somebody *might* know what happened to the money because he did have a few men passengers. And of course they had a good chance to grab up any money that might be handy, or it might have been someone who helped to get it up.

I don't know anything about that. I don't know whether Victor does— probably not, either. I don't think *that* investigation ever got anywhere except to call it a disaster. Nobody could understand it, knowing how well that captain knew the Creek, and even if it wasn't a very clear night, he'd been there so often that I think he could have gone there with his eyes closed. *(Victor: The* Alert *is still there. Gordon and Brian [Victor's sons] dived on it with SCUBA gear. It lies mostly on its side. Earl said Larson was reported to have been found floating in the Creek several days later.)*

Alice: Then you don't really know that he was drunk or that he was even conscious when the boat went over?

Augusta: We don't know. Nobody knows.

Alice: Somebody might have been after the money to start with?

Augusta: That's just supposition, or that somebody tried to make him drunk—something like that—or gave him something. It might have been in some kind of a drink to make him drowsy, sleepy, or even worse. Nobody ever has really found out exactly what happened, except that I think they did get the boat up, and it wasn't very much good then after it had been there. Let's ask Victor; he may remember. *(Victor: Earl was told that Larson had stopped at the Weaver place, just west of our property, where a woman made and sold moonshine. They didn't actually raise the boat. Dan Baxley got a cable onto the cabin trying to raise it but only pulled off part of it.)*

Alice: I know Victor knows a lot about that because he told me about sounding along there from his boat, looking for things.

Augusta: Yes, I think that although he wasn't there at the time—that was before his day—he's heard so much about all of it, I'm sure.

Alice: Okay, then let's go on to the trips to Green Cove Springs. It was easier to get to Jacksonville than it was to get to Green Cove then, wasn't it?

Augusta: Not really easier, because to Jacksonville it was a four-hour trip each way—that is, you spent the day, practically, on the water, and then about two hours in Jacksonville, but the rest of the time you were on the river and Creek, either going or coming back. And when we went to Green Cove, we had to drive the ten miles over very sandy roads, which made that drive slow. You couldn't expect horses to pull even just a buggy through sand very quickly. And that would always take us the better part of an hour really to get there.

Alice: That's all?

Augusta: Yes, well that's enough time for a horse, I think.

Alice: I would think it would take longer than that because it used to take us half an hour with the car when the road was still all sand.

Augusta, Marguerite, Marie, and Max Pflug could make the trip to Green Cove Springs in a little more than an hour with the horse and wagon. Purchase of their Model T Ford cut that time to about half an hour.

Max, Raymond Hendricks, and Marie in Max's new Model T Ford

Augusta: Well, if it's half an hour with a car, a horse should be able to make it in maybe twice the time. Well, anyway, it was a long drive, but it doesn't seem that it was much over an hour, although I do know that even when we thought we were getting quite an early start, we'd get there sometimes at noon when they closed the stores.

In Green Cove Springs, they would close almost everything at noon, from noon to one for some places, noon to two for others. They had a long closing time at noon. If you wanted to go, for instance, to the courthouse, you couldn't really do anything if you got there about noon. You'd just have to wait. But we had all kinds of shopping here and there to do, and I know that we often got there when some of the places where we wanted to go—the bank and such—had closed for noon, and they'd open again in the afternoon.

Then when we got home, it would often be pretty late in the afternoon. So it was a whole day's trip—just about as it was to Jacksonville. And then after we did get to Green Cove, we couldn't get a lot of the things we wanted.

I'll tell you one store I didn't like to go to, and that was Miss Watkins's father's store. It was a meat market, and unfortunately there was always a lot of fish. And there was always such an awful smell in that store. I guess he had things open, but he had too much in the way of "perfume." I used to hate to go in there. But we did buy meat there.

Alice: Well, he was the only butcher, wasn't he?

Augusta: He was the only one who had a special meat store. They'd have meat in other stores, but he was the only one that had special things.

Alice: Is that the one that was later Stuart's Meat Market? Or was that a totally different store? I remember when I was growing up we always went to Stuart's Meat Market.

Augusta: I think that was a different store. I don't think that had anything to do with it.

Alice: It was right on the main street.

Augusta: I don't think it was the same at all, although I wouldn't swear to that. It appears to me that it was something different. At that time, then, we didn't buy meat at Stuart's. That's the reason I can't quite remember now about that, but after Mr. Watkins was gone, we bought all our meat somewhere else. Now I don't know just where.

Is there anything else now about the trips?

Alice: Yes, how about the way you got home many weekends when you were teaching in Spring Glen?

Augusta: Oh, that was something!

On Friday afternoons, I would ride my bicycle from where I was boarding in Spring Glen to South Jacksonville, leave my bicycle there, take the ferry across the Saint Johns River to Jacksonville, take a passenger boat down the Saint Johns and Black Creek to our dock, where my parents would meet me.

I would usually bring some groceries and some dessert so that we wouldn't have to do much cooking for the Sunday dinner.

Then, when I went back on Sunday, my parents would take me in their boat to the railroad bridge across Black Creek near Russell. I would get on the train, which would stop if it was signaled, ride to Jacksonville, take the ferry across to South Jacksonville, get my bicycle, and ride back to where I was boarding in Spring Glen.

Now, is there anything else about traveling?

Alice: Can you think of anything else? Of course you've told me about the spring in Green Cove being such a tourist attraction.

Augusta: Oh, yes, of course, especially in those days to the people who didn't have cars, which, of course, was almost everybody. There were very few cars. Supposing you mention this—that in 1911 the only place in Green Cove where you could even order a car was—

Alice: Don't tell me it was Gustafson's! Not way back then!

Augusta: It *was* Gustafson's—the present milk company. At that time, they had the livery stable there. One branch of the family went into auto sales. They weren't selling any milk then. They got all those cows later. They had the livery stable, and they were renting horses, too. That is, if you wanted to rent a horse to ride, or if you wanted to rent one to pull a wagon or something, they would have horses there. It was just a regular livery stable, and their descendants run the dairy now. *(Alice: There is still a*

77

photo of "Ma and Pa Gus" on some of the dairy's milk cartons in 2014, and the company delivers chocolate milk for the University of Florida football team.)

Alice: And that's where you got your Ford?

Augusta: I guess my father ordered it through them. I'm not sure, but I know that 1917 Ford we had was one of the very first passenger automobiles in Clay County. I just wish I could remember numbers as well as Victor can, but it does seem to me that the price was about three hundred dollars. It may have been a little over but not much. And it had to be sent on special order from Detroit.

Isn't that where they make autos now? The Ford people? You know, they had those Model Ts. Of course it was a Ford, and it was still the kind that had curtains you had to put down when it rained. By the time you had the curtains down, the rain would probably be all over. And of course in winter when it was very cold, the only way you could keep a little bit of the wind out was those curtains. The tires were awfully poor at that time—very poor.

My brother thought it would be so much fun that summer, after we had the Ford here, if our parents would let us, and they said all right if we wanted to risk it, to drive up and get Auntie. She was up there in Virginia, in Bristol, teaching at Virginia Intermont College.

Oscar loved to drive. That was something new, and he thought it would be a nice trip for him and me, and then for her coming back, if we went up there to meet her and then brought her home instead of having her come on the train for her vacation. It was about time for her to come back anyway. So we did go up there, and you may have heard me say that my brother changed tires many times; it seemed like every hour or so we had a flat tire. The tires were poor, *and* the roads were poor.

One of the hazards encountered when Oscar and Augusta drove to Bristol, Virginia

Alice: How long did it take you to make that trip?

Augusta: Three days. Of course, we didn't drive all that time. We didn't drive at night at all. Every night we stopped somewhere. But there weren't even any motels then.

Alice: That must have been kind of scary through the mountains.

Augusta: Well, of course that was just the very last part, where we had to go through the mountains.

Alice: But it's an important part.

Augusta: Yes. Well, we made it.

As I remember it, my brother was a very careful driver. He really tried to take very good care of the car, too. I know he promised my father that he would, and my father knew that he would do that. We made it up there and back, but both ways it took three days because we always stopped before dark. In that way, each day we drove just in the daylight hours. I don't think that it could possibly have been less expensive than coming some other way because of all the tires we had to buy, because we couldn't stop and wait to have anything repaired.

I don't really know how all that worked about the tires, but maybe some of the tires could be patched up right then and there some way. But I know we got home all right, and that trip taught us at the time that in the future it would be all right to make long automobile trips, but we realized that it wasn't yet that time.

Alice: What about your brother, my Uncle Oscar? Could you tell me some more about him, because I don't know much at all about him?

Augusta: He had kind of an interesting career. I guess you know that he was three years younger than I. So he would now be—

Alice: Auntie was the youngest, wasn't she?

Augusta: No, he was the youngest. I was, of course, the oldest, and my sister was two years younger, and my brother three years younger. So he would now be eighty-seven, but he died when he was thirty-seven. Mind you, that many years ago! And he died on a business trip.

But to go back further than that, my brother was in a military school for several years. My father thought that a military school was good training for boys. He knew they'd be strict. And my father thought that it was a very good thing for a boy to be in a school that was strict and made him do his work and made him do exercises. So my brother really had some military training right there in a military school in Germany. (*Alice: Appendix 6 suggests that he also attended a military school in New Jersey.*)

Oscar Pflug in World War I US Army uniform

Of course all of us could speak English well because we children learned it very quickly, and my parents already knew some English, and they learned it quickly, too. We children learned it without accents. And then when my father went back to Germany on business, it was in the years before World War I. I think you have it written somewhere that we first came to the US in 1898. And then the first time we went back to Germany was in 1905.

Oscar served in the US Army in World War I. After he left the army, he got a job with the Vacuum Oil Company, part of the Tidewater Oil Company. It was a good job for him with cars becoming so much in demand, and he kept it until he died on a business trip when they had sent him to Japan in

1929. That's when it must have been because my father died in 1919, and my brother's death was ten years later.

He was cremated when he died suddenly in Japan. We were told that he had a kidney ailment and that it got worse quickly. I don't know if they could have done more for him here. Maybe so. Anyway, he died right there in Japan, and that was sad for my mother. You know, my father had died ten years before.

Marie was with Auntie at the time in Bristol, just waiting and waiting to hear from my brother because he was good about writing at least once a week, and she hadn't heard from him for some time—much longer than usual. She was getting worried, and I know my sister told me that in Bristol at her college apartment, she—Auntie—was coming downstairs one day, and there was our mother standing by a window by the stairs, looking terribly unhappy, and my sister asked her, "What in the world is the matter?" She thought she was sick. And my mother said that she had just had a message from the Vacuum Oil Company, for whom my brother was working, that he had died and that they had cremated him and were shipping him to New York to the company there. They buried him in Cypress Hill National Cemetery on Long Island because he had—now let's see—where does the "military" come in?

Alice: Well, I thought that because of his military school training in Germany he was taken into the US Army as an officer. (*Alice: I was mistaken. He entered the army as a private in 1918, but attained the rank of second lieutenant when he was discharged in 1920.*)

Augusta: Yes. And he advanced there pretty well. But you see that was awfully hard on my mother because she had depended on him so much, and also for sustenance, because he was giving her a certain amount every month. There was no social security then. And of course my father had left a certain amount but not enough for her to live on the rest of her life. (*Alice: My grandmother suspected that Oscar was murdered, but we have no proof that such a thing occurred.*)

Alice: And he was married then to—Katherine?

Augusta: Oh, I—

Alice: Bobby's mother?

Augusta: Goodness, I can't even think of her name. You know I have to stop to think who is whose mother.

Alice: Yes, of course.

Augusta: I get all you folks mixed up now. I have to stop and think—Alice Marie—two boys, one girl—married to Ralph. And then there's Victor with his two boys and Carmen. And then there's Gerald with Gladys and—now whose name am I trying to think of?

Alice: Well, Gerald has the three children—David, Terry, and Suzy.

Augusta: I mean who was it we were trying to think of?

Alice: Oh, okay. Bobby's mother was Katherine? Bobby's mother—your brother's wife?

Augusta: Bobby—yes. Bobby's mother had several sisters, and they were all trying to raise Bobby—and that's what made him kind of sissy, I think— that he had no man around as he was growing up in the family, just all those women folks. But now you're asking for—

Alice: His mother's name.

Augusta: Anne. Anne Evers.

Alice: And Aunt Katherine is the one who survived his mother? And she took care of him the last few years he was home?

Augusta: Yes, and there was still another aunt. I don't really know all those sisters' names. But anyway, it's Anne—yes. Now is there any other question that I might have an hour wondering about?

Alice: Let's see, Uncle Oscar had some connection with Eddie Rickenbacker, somewhere. Was that in the oil company? Remember that picture you used to have upstairs in Grandma's room of him standing by Rickenbacker's racing car?

Augusta: I don't even remember the picture very well.

Alice: I know it was a great big, powerful car.

Augusta: And you thought my brother had something to do with it?

Alice: I thought that he did, yes, with Rickenbacker.

Augusta: Please ask Victor about that because I certainly don't remember. I remember the name, but that's all. There were lots of things in which I was not too interested, and I just can't remember. (*Alice: According to the* Dipstick, *the Newsletter of the Tidewater MG Classics Car Club, "The famous World War One Air Ace Eddie Rickenbacker drove his modified Duesenberg all over the U.S.A, winning various awards," during the 1920s when Oscar was employed with Tidewater and Vacuum Oil. http://www. mg.org/Dipstick/2007 issues/March 2007.pdf*)

Alice: I will ask Victor. But Uncle Oscar did spend some time here then? Here on this place?

Augusta: He spent no time except visiting. He visited occasionally, not very often, but he visited occasionally and liked it very much and enjoyed the Creek. I know he liked that! The swimming and the boating he liked, but he didn't like the location out here. He thought we were too far from anywhere. And there were very few paved roads at that time, so you can understand that. It was bad driving.

Alice: What was his position in that company? And where did Tidewater Oil come into the story?

Augusta: Well, that's a big company, and I think it still is called Tidewater Oil Company. He was evidently one whom they sent out to visit customers and somewhat like a traveling salesman, I suppose. They always sent him because they thought that he was well able to get business in. *(Victor: He worked for J. Paul Getty making contacts for Socony Vacuum Oil in the Orient. Through mergers and takeovers, Socony Vacuum became a part of what is now Exxon/Mobil.)*

When we have a chance and you want to listen, I must play you the record from an album that Auntie sent that has the name "Oscar" on it. And the funny thing about that is that it says on that record that the "Oscar" of the song was "liebling der Frauen" (a darling of the women) "ist Oscar bekannt" (Oscar is known). "Bei ihn sind die Maedchen wie Wax in die Hand" (With him the girls are like wax in the hand).

That struck me so funny because Oscar was always very popular with the girls, and he was so different from Bobby, his son. He was always making friends, and he was very outgoing, while Bobby, as I hear and as we notice, since he doesn't even write to us, is just the opposite. But Oscar and my father were the outgoing ones.

A funny episode that I remember well was one night when my mother and father came to the room where the three of us were playing to tell us good night before they left for some dinner or something for which they were all dressed up. After they had said good night and turned to leave, Oscar said loudly, "Mama, you look nice from the back!" My mother and father got a good laugh out of that.

Now my father and my mother were quite different in temperament. She was more as I am. I don't care to go out much. I'll go to dinner with you tonight, but really, I don't care about it that much, and I know every once in a while all these folks that come here invite me, or say they would like to invite me to go out to dinner with them, and I tell them—and this is the truth—that I would rather eat at home. I don't know if that's a pleasant thing to tell people. Now that doesn't mean, Alice Marie, that I don't like to eat at your house, but it's simply that I would rather stay at home. Maybe you understand that now.

If you will just remember—Oscar was quite different from me, and he was a very great favorite in that company. I know that my mother had letters from people who had worked in that oil company with him in the office, and they were just so sad about his not coming back. Or coming back but only cremated. That was just a sad time.

Alice: Yes, I should think so.

Oscar with spanish moss

Augusta: And then of course it was a sad time for my mother with my father gone and then Oscar gone, and of course she and your father never did get along well together.

Alice: I can remember that. Victor said something about Grandma's insisting that Daddy change from his work clothes for meals, and he didn't like that. I don't blame him much.

Augusta: I don't think she actually meant that he should dress up, but, you know, just kind of fix himself up a little bit. Maybe if he had on an open shirt to button it.

No, I'm sorry that they didn't get along better. I think it was a fault of both of them, but I think chiefly of my mother. She should have been nicer to him, I think. But then, she didn't think that he was doing enough for me. She was still of that era when women didn't really work, and I was one of the first married women that taught. You know, in most places they do take married women now, but for a while they didn't even want married women because they said they'd always have babies or have to be home with the children. I think that was one of the reasons she didn't approve—she thought I ought to be home with the children. Naturally, she was left with you sometimes and your brothers. And it just was a little difficult at times.

Alice: I can see that. I remember her, but I don't remember her too clearly when she was still well. It's too bad they didn't get along better.

Augusta: I don't think you remember her when she was still herself, really.

One day she was in the car with Earl driving. She was complaining loudly about his hitting bumps and making her migraine headache worse. Just then, he hit a really bad bump, and she hit her head on the side of the car and turned to berate him but stopped suddenly and said, "My headache is gone!" He had cured her migraine!

Marie and Earl in porch swing

And I'm sure you remember that she kept all the beautiful German china packed away in the steamer trunk in her room, don't you? She felt it was too good to use. After she died, we did use it for special occasions, and still do. It seemed a shame to keep it where no one could see it and enjoy it.

Alice: I'm glad you did take it out. I remember when Daddy made the corner china closet for you to have it on display. It was very thoughtful of him to do that.

I can remember when I was very little being with her in the kitchen and watching her make a cake. And I can remember other times playing on the floor in the kitchen while she was cooking or doing something there. And I remember that she was terrified of spiders and thunderstorms. We had to close the windows and all sit in the dining room until a storm was over. It was stiflingly hot until we could open the windows again after the storm and let in the cool air.

Augusta: One thing I can understand now and couldn't so much at the time, since I've had to take care of little ones, was that your father would be outside working on something—cars, maybe—out there at his shop, and the rest of us would be in school.

You'd be home here with your grandma, and she always told me that she had such a hard time keeping track of you because you would slip out. You liked to be with your father out there at his workshop. But you know that is kind of worrisome when you have a small child to look after, and you go back to the bedroom or some place and come back, and the child's gone. Well, she'd go out there, and usually she'd find you with your dad, but she didn't like that because she wanted you to stay here at the house when she was responsible for you. She didn't want you to go out there when she wasn't sure you were with him.

Alice: But what he was doing was *so* much more interesting than what she was doing. I can remember that.

Augusta: Oh, I can see why you would go out there with him. I think you and your dad—you got along just fine, especially when you were little. You were very fond of him, and he of you, of course, and I think that was what made trouble about Grandma. Then maybe she scolded you for going out and told him that she wanted you to stay in here. He probably told her that he didn't mind if you came out there. He liked to have you around. But of course I can see now that if I were left with a small child and the small child would run out somewhere, when I didn't know where he or she had gone, that would be worrisome. And once or twice it even worried me when I was home and you had suddenly disappeared. What you liked to do was to go down to the "Shady Lane." Do you remember that? *(Alice: "Shady Lane" was our name for a path Earl had cut through heavy woods paralleling the little stream that flowed past our house to the Creek.)*

Alice: Oh, yes. I remember that, too.

Augusta: You enjoyed the Shady Lane, and I was afraid that you might get somewhere where there were snakes or something you shouldn't be in. We have sometimes had some of the grandchildren here, and you know I can remember now that some of them would bear watching, too.

Alice: But I never did get bitten by a snake.

Augusta: I'm glad you didn't. But you know it could have happened, and of course there were other things that wouldn't have been so pleasant.

Alice: Well, let's see what else I have down here in my notes. Victor mentioned some of these people the other day that were with Mr. Staub out in the Staub House—Schneeberger and Robinson. *(Alice: Mr. Staub, from Pennsylvania, spent several winters occupying a little house on our property, up near the gate, hence its name, "the Staub house.")*

Henry Clay Staub (left) and his friends loved fishing on Black Creek.

Augusta: Yes, those were friends, of course, of Mr. Staub, and they had come to Florida for fishing and so forth. And since they knew that Mr. Staub was here, they came by to see him.

Alice: And then he mentioned McGowan. I remember hearing that name, too.

Augusta: I guess he was right with that crowd. (*Victor: No, he stayed in the Staub house during a time when Staub was not there.*)

Alice: He's the one that Victor told me had buried something out there. He said that he saw him burying something.

Augusta: He didn't remember what it was—maybe an animal?

Alice: No, no. He was sure it was money of some kind. But Victor told me yesterday that McGowan was a sort of ne'er-do-well type that just worked a little bit and not much and wouldn't do any more than he had to.

Augusta: I remember very little about him.

Alice: He was supposed to be helping around the place, Victor said.

Augusta: Helping us?

Alice: Yes.

Augusta: I must ask Victor about that again and see what else he remembers. See, I wasn't home too much myself when I was teaching.

Alice: Then he mentioned the McLaughlins again. I remember that—"Mr. McTeeny-TinyLaughlin" and "Mr. McOtherLaughlin." He said they were at Irving's boarding house in Jacksonville when you were staying there. (*Alice: After the stillbirth of Hugh Gordon Thorp in 1922, Augusta went to stay close to Riverside Hospital in Jacksonville when the time was near for each subsequent birth.*)

Augusta: Mr. McOtherLaughlin! That *was* funny!

Alice: And then he also mentioned Wilhelmina, who took care of him in Orange Park. She was the girlfriend of a chauffeur. (*Alice: I believe he was the DuPont family's chauffeur. The DuPonts owned a beautiful estate on the river in Orange Park. The Orange Park school children were once invited to see their tulip garden in bloom.*)

Augusta: It's all so long ago I can barely remember them, but I do remember that Victor was always funny about the names he remembered and how he remembered them. But can you remember—no, I guess it was before your time—when Mr. Staub had four friends come and stay with him?

Alice: No, I don't remember that.

Augusta: You don't remember that, of course, but Mr. Staub must have been here altogether eight years or so—in succession, I think. At least that. It was sort of the time between you and Victor. I mean you are eight years apart. It was somewhere in that time that Mr. Staub had four friends come, and he asked if it would be all right for him to have them out there at the Staub house. We told him we didn't have cots or anything to give them. He said never mind, he would just get moss.

Alice: Oh, my!

Augusta: And he got a lot of moss and just covered the floor with moss, and I don't even know if they had anything to put over that. We didn't have a whole lot of stuff to give them, especially the way it would be treated out there. We didn't want to give them any good sheets or blankets or anything. Mr. Staub said they didn't really need anything. It was warm weather. Not really hot, but it wasn't too cold, either.

Alice: Weren't there a few things that came in with the moss? Like redbugs?

Augusta: Oh, gosh. I wouldn't even begin to wonder what was in that moss! You know, nothing very big of course, but in the way of smaller insects and so on. Anyway, he brought all that moss in. I think he had some sacks, too, for pillows that he filled with moss. We didn't worry about that. *We* hadn't invited those people, so it was up to Mr. Staub to provide for them.

What I was afraid of even at that time, and now think of even more so, is that they certainly must have had some alcohol. Something to drink. They probably had quite a bit of beer out there, or whatever. Anyway, nothing happened, really, but they would all go fishing or at least try to catch fish.

Mr. Staub was very good at catching fish, and I think they all lived more or less on fish. Then, of course, they really had no way to go anywhere, but I know they must have managed the groceries some way. I don't know whether we got them some or what. I wasn't even home much during that time, so I don't know too much about it, but that was the one time, I think, that it was a little bit too much. It was all right to have Mr. Staub there, but I think that he was probably asked not to have anyone else come.

They were all Moose—you know at Orange Park they had Moose Haven? *(Alice: Moose Haven was opened in 1922 by the Moose, a fraternal organization, for a retirement home.)* And that's really the way Mr. Staub came out here, you know. He got acquainted with us because he wanted a place where he could go and fish, and someone in Orange Park told him about us. So that's the way we got together. But Mr. Staub liked to be here. He liked it very much. And only that one time he had all those fellows here, and then he was told, "No, not anymore!"

Alice: And each year when he went back to Pennsylvania, he sent us some maple sugar candy.

Augusta: Yes.

Alice: I remember that. And I also remember that you told me he liked to make his coffee with Creek water.

Augusta: Oh, gracious, yes. You know for several years, we still had the bathhouse down there at the Creek. And that, of course, was screened, and the screen door could be hooked, and we had two cots in there.

Alice: And scorpions! We always had to shake the scorpions out of our bathing suits before we put them on when they'd been hanging in there.

Marguerite and friend

Augusta: I don't know what all else besides the scorpions, but those cots did have some old mattresses. Anyway, it was fixed up for a place to sleep, and Auntie and her friend, Mary Crenshaw, slept there one summer during their vacation. She and Mary were the first ones who slept there, and then another year Mr. Staub and whoever. I think he was probably there alone most of the time. He cooked down there sometimes, and he evidently liked it here very much because he came until he got really sick and couldn't travel anymore, and then he soon died—or so we heard.

Alice: I remember something I heard about his coffee—that he started out with one batch of grounds and used the same grounds, just added to them, all winter long?

Augusta: No, it wasn't exactly that way, but the fact is that he had friends up there in Philadelphia who sold coffee. When he came to Florida, I suppose he asked for it maybe, or they voluntarily gave it to him. Anyway, when he was coming to Florida, they would give him a great big amount of coffee, but it was coffee that we didn't buy. You don't know much about coffee, and I don't know too much myself except a few things that I like—you know—Nescafe and Sanka and Maxwell House, that's what I have now. But Mr. Staub must have liked that coffee.

Anyway, I suppose when you are given a lot, you'd better like it and use it. He came with that amount of coffee, and then when he was ready to leave one year, he gave us what was left of his coffee. You know, we fixed that coffee one time, and that was all we wanted. We just didn't like the taste of it at all. I think it had a lot of chicory in it. We didn't do anything with it but throw it away. We just couldn't even use it. But he evidently liked it very much and used it all the time, because he never had us get any coffee for him when we bought his other groceries.

Also, when those friends were here, I should hope they would at least have helped him with the food, because, you know, we didn't feed them. We didn't invite them all to dinner or anything like that. We weren't going to start anything like that, although we did usually have Mr. Staub in every Sunday for dinner when he was here alone, and I think that was the only real meal he ever ate during the week. I know he wouldn't want to cook much; and of course he always had fish. When his friends were here, they caught a lot of fish, and I imagine they ate a lot of fish.

Alice: I think we have pictures of them in the albums in the den. I remember seeing a picture of a big string of fish that they had caught. I guess that's when the four of them were here.

Augusta: We'll have to look at some of those old pictures sometime. Now can you think of anything else that "forgetful me" might be able to remember?

Alice: I'm trying.

Augusta: Well, if anything comes to you, Victor might know.

Alice: What I'm trying to do is get the histories before the time Victor and I can remember, and then maybe we can fill in from there. And Gerald, of course, too. But mostly those early days are the things that are so interesting to everybody.

Augusta: Yes, and that was before the time of all of you.

Alice: In the early days here in Florida, you didn't have any refrigeration, did you?

Augusta: No, we had no refrigeration. There was no electricity, and if we went to get ice, of course we came home with *some* ice, but you can imagine—a slow trip from Green Cove?

Alice: I imagine, with the horse and buggy, you wouldn't even try?

Augusta: Well, yes, we did. We had a sort of icebox thing. After you got your ice in that, it would stay fairly protected, but we'd certainly not get home with the amount with which we started, but that's the only way we'd bring ice. And we quite frequently made ice cream in those days, so you know we must have had some ice.

Alice: I can remember our having ice cream when I was growing up. Gerald would hand crank it.

Augusta: And we made our ice cream. Well, I don't know what else would be interesting at that time.

Alice: Just about anything is, really, because there are so few people that would remember it accurately or even remember it at all. Particularly the way you got around and the way you met with people and so on.

Augusta: Well, in those days, of course, the biggest trouble always was roads. You know that other place over there to the east, before the Linstedts bought this part and built our old house? It was just old Mrs. Chesser that lived over there in the past, about in the spot where the Boones built their house. Of course her little old house was torn down long ago. But they were so provoked—I mean the neighbors around here—when my father had this whole place fenced in.

There was a time, right at the beginning, when he had a fence built around the entire thirty acres. And then he planted 144 pecan trees, and you know about those—twelve rows of each—Stuart, Bradley, President, and such.

And when old Mrs. Chesser lived over there, I think she lived there alone, but all these other Chessers were her children or grandchildren that lived around here. They had been used to coming over to see her, and they had a shortcut from about where the Silcoxes are now. From there on, there was a shortcut right over to her house. Of course in between there—you know, up there where that very wet place is, and the pond—they could, naturally, go around it on our property until my father had that fence built, and then that part was shut off, and they didn't like that a bit.

So first thing we knew, there had been pieces cut out of the fence, and the Chessers were coming through again. My father would have the fence mended, and you can imagine how long it stayed mended. Then in the end, a lot of it was stolen. There was still a piece of fence when the Raymond Hendricks house was up there. You know where that house was that is also torn down now.

Well, you see, all the relatives, when they came to see Grandma Chesser over here, could take that shortcut. And you can imagine how they felt when that was shut off, and they had to go the wet way around through a whole lot of really bad, muddy mess up there. That was one reason why that fence just gradually disappeared. I think even now there are places people would like to go through. I don't know.

But Jordan *(a neighbor)* has to watch out all the time that nobody settles in over there in what's left of that house. You know about the time that somebody had started to cook in there? So you see, there was that temptation to cut a fence out of the way if you wanted to get somewhere.

Alice: Or if you wanted to let your animals in to graze a bit.

Augusta: Oh, and that's another thing—please remember—if Victor *ever* talks about raising cattle, you tell him that I said, "Please don't!" Because if you don't grow up with animals, you're not going to be a bit of good making them a business. It seems easy enough to make a fence and keep your cows in there, but you're not going to keep them in there long. People are going to cut your fence and let your cows out. You know what trouble Jordan has now with keeping his hogs in.

Alice: I'll bet that's because hogs are so smart.

Augusta: I can tell you that cows are smart enough to get out if they want to. And, of course if Victor ever should start with cows, he might have hogs, too.

Alice: I doubt it.

When you first got here, the pump was way out, wasn't it? Or was it in the house then? (*Alice: This was a hand pump for water. There was no running water in the house until the late 1940s.*)

Augusta: Well, no. When we first came—when the old house was there—there was a hand pump on the back porch, and there was a well, of course, underneath that. That's where we got our water for a while, and then that other well was dug—farther out because this well was sort of going to the bad. During those first days, we still had a well somewhere with a hand pump, and those are the two I remember the best. There might possibly have been one out somewhere with the sheds, but that wouldn't be so important.

The well that you remember was a big, deep hole in the ground with a section of the hollow trunk of a cypress tree topped with a cover and a pitcher pump attached to the pipe down to the aquifer. There were two very large clumps of bamboo shading the well area where we did the laundry. Victor and Gerald had to go down into the well quite often to remove the bamboo roots that would almost fill it up. And do you remember when a snake fell into the well through a hole on the side and died? We had to carry water from a well at Russell until Victor and Gerald could go down into the well to see what was wrong. They found and removed the dead snake and pumped out all the bad-tasting, smelly water.

Alice: Who could *ever* forget that! We first thought the bad taste and smell might be just an excess of bamboo roots.

Where did all that bamboo come from, anyway? We had two big ones at the gate, two big ones by the well, and two down the path to the "Bamboo." (*Alice: That's what we euphemistically called our outhouse because it was hidden behind two of the bamboo bushes.*)

Augusta: Oscar brought some tiny shoots of bamboo back from the Orient one time, and it grew a little too well!

Of course there was always water needed while we had a horse or a mule or a cow or whatever. They had to be given water. Then about the time Grandma died—in the forties anyway—it must have been—suppose you say about '45—an artesian well was dug, and you know how it's dug—they just put down the pipe. We had that man come with his rig—I don't remember what his name was now.

Alice: I don't remember, either. (*Victor: It was Hardenbrook.*)

Augusta: Anyway, he dug the artesian well, and do you know that Victor said that at Fellowship Park they had to go deeper for an artesian well than here? Anyway, that's what provided the water supply. You might mention that Mr. Staub, our visitor from Pennsylvania, always declared that for drinking and for making coffee, Black Creek water was the best. The water that *I* think was really the best for drinking was from the well, though. A glass filled with cold water from that well on a hot summer day was wonderful. When there were no snakes in it, of course, but that happened only once. But Mr. Staub did like the Creek water better than any other.

Alice: I agree about the good taste and coldness of the well water.

I suppose Mr. Staub liked the Creek for bathing, too?

Augusta: He didn't mention that especially. Of course for drinking and fishing, he liked the water in Black Creek, but I don't know how often he actually went in swimming because he was here mostly in winter.

Alice: I remember that electricity came the first year I was away at FSU. That would have been late 1949 or early 1950.

Augusta: And that was all after the time that Grandma was sick and then died in 1946.

Alice: The electricity was after Grandma died. I remember that you sold some timber for each of those acquisitions. You sold just enough to pay for the well and just enough to pay for the electrical wiring.

Augusta: Yes, and also I sold enough timber for the telephone line as well. You know Baxley was the one who bought that lumber. Grandma had always not wanted any trees cut at all, so any that I had Baxley cut while she was still here, I had him cut where it wouldn't even show. I don't think most people would even have noticed any trees gone.

Alice: No, I don't think so, but I didn't really think much cutting was done while she was still here.

Augusta: I'm sure she was. I know that I did it then because I felt we needed some of those things. Let's see now, when she was sick, didn't we already have the telephone?

Alice: Oh, no. The telephone didn't come until Daddy died in 1961. You were living alone then, and we wanted you to have some contact with the outside world and especially with us.

Augusta: That was later, then.

Alice: Yes.

Augusta: The electricity had to be here then. It just seems to me that Grandma didn't cook on anything but that old stove.

Alice: Right, she didn't cook on anything but the kerosene stove. And of course for the last few years she wasn't cooking anyway. But I remember coming home from college and finding the wiring and another time finding a bathroom fixed up. You and Gerald fixed that, too. Finally we had a real indoor bathroom with running water!

Augusta: And then, of course, the refrigerator came in there somewhere. Do you remember?

Alice: I remember you had a small refrigerator in the old house, and then also one in this house.

Augusta: Well, it seems to me that there for a while I just had that timber cut and always showed them where to cut, and told them not to cut anywhere near the road where it showed.

Alice: I know that Auntie objected, too, to having timber cut. She objected to having things left, like pieces of trees left out there.

Augusta: Yes, I know.

Another time, there was lots of moss growing in the pecan trees, and do you happen to remember that colored man who with his boys—

Alice: "Holmes" was his name, I think.

Augusta: The man from Green Cove, and he and his sons—they were teenagers—got up into the trees and freed the pecan trees of a great deal of spanish moss.

Alice: That was during the forties, too, I think. I remember that we tried to get as much moss as possible down with long bamboo poles, but that wasn't very efficient.

Augusta: I'm quite sure that's when Grandma was still here, partly because she didn't object to that at all—getting the moss out of the trees. It was just the cutting of trees that she objected to. Have we already said that Mr. Staub made beds of spanish moss?

Alice: Yes, for his "guests."

Augusta: Let's see if there is anything else about Mr. Staub. There were all kinds of strange things. Let's see if I can remember anything else. I guess you'd said something about his living on fish.

Alice: Yes, you mentioned that yesterday.

Augusta: He just drank coffee and ate fish, and I think that's all about his diet, except for the Sunday dinners for which we invited him.

Alice: I wonder why he did that. Was he really that hard up, or did you even know that much about him?

Augusta: Oh, he wasn't hard up. (*Victor: I believe Staub was part owner of the* Meyersdale Republican, *a weekly newspaper in his hometown in Pennsylvania.*)

Alice: He just liked roughing it?

Augusta: I have no idea how much money he had, but we always had the conviction that he and his family had plenty of money. He had been working for the railroad, and they were well paid even then. And he may even have had a pension when he retired. I don't remember that, if I was ever told. I didn't care, you know—it wasn't anything I would ask about, but I do know that he had plenty of money. We were all convinced of that, and that's why it was so funny that he'd spend only about two dollars a week on his food, and that was just about all he spent here.

Alice: I guess he did just like roughing it.

Augusta: He liked it. That was comfortable enough for him, and he just loved to be on the Creek fishing. He loved that. And he loved to be out of doors, or he wouldn't have come back all those years, but he might not have made eight or nine winters in Florida without being here—not really paying for anything but his food.

Alice: I imagine he got a break on the trip down for being an ex-railway employee. Probably even got to ride free.

Augusta: Oh, he probably did get something—a special fare, maybe. I wouldn't be surprised. Oh, no, he wasn't hard up by any means.

Alice: Did he get mail while he was here?

Augusta: I'm sure he got mail, but I can't remember that he got much mail. What made you wonder if he got mail?

Alice: I was just curious because you said that you were surprised when you found out he had two daughters.

Augusta: They didn't write, I guess. I don't think he was in touch with them or whoever his former wife was. No, I don't think—I *know* it wasn't much mail—sometimes advertisements and stuff were forwarded to him. But he never really spoke to us, not even to your father, about his life. For a long time, he didn't say a word about any family or even say a word about having been married, except once or twice something slipped out about "son-in-law." We were wondering how in the world a man who hadn't been married would have a son-in-law.

Alice: So he was divorced then? Not a widower?

Augusta: I don't know if he was even divorced. Anyway, he certainly was separated. He was living, as we understood it, with some members of his family, and his family, I think, may have been some sisters or maybe a brother or so—but anyway, the immediate family, not some wife's folks or any children at all, except then he told your father about having children. I guess that must have come about, too, when something might even have been said about grandchildren. I don't know. Any way it was, your father surmised he did see his daughters maybe once in a while. He just didn't want to talk to any of the rest of us about any past.

Alice: Well, that was his privilege, of course. It would be nice, I think, to be able to go off somewhere like that and not have anybody know anything about you and not have to answer questions.

Augusta: He certainly was lucky to be able to stay on this place because that just suited him. Before he came out here and even got acquainted with us, I think he had been in Orange Park at least once during the winter, maybe, but not so long as he was afterward out here. But that's where he got in with the Moose and the general country around Orange Park, anyway. And he was just simply not exactly what you could call a family man.

Alice: Okay, enough for him.

You just reminded me of something else. That was the kind of entertainment that they had at the schools then. You know, they don't do that much anymore. They don't usually have people coming in like I remember at Orange Park. Remember the man with the trick horse came, and Koko the Clown, and the magician, and the revivalists, and a number of others? We had all those different people coming and giving assembly programs for the school?

Augusta: But you see one reason for that was that most local people couldn't go to the programs if the programs were somewhere else. So they were more interested in having someone come to them at the school. Now they wouldn't even care about some of those programs. That was, I guess, *all* the schools, not only the country schools but *all* the schools. I mean also Green Cove Springs, which already had a high school. I imagine they had entertainment in all the schools. I know they did in the small schools.

Alice: I don't remember it in Green Cove so much.

Augusta: Well, maybe not when you went there.

Alice: It seems to me that when I went there, most of the entertainment was what we produced ourselves. Maybe if I think more about it, I'll remember some, but I do remember how we enjoyed those things that came to the Orange Park School. The magician had such a scary show. And remember that trick horse that ate some woman's flowers off her hat? It was fun for all us kids. And also, so many people have remarked to you that they enjoyed the auditorium programs every Friday, with singing, when you were principal at Orange Park. That was when I was in school there, too, in first, second, and third grades.

Augusta: Yes. Once a week, we'd go into the auditorium on a Friday morning, and we'd sing together. The whole school. And I think we changed off having different grades present something, didn't we? For instance, have the primary grades do something and another teacher's pupils perform.

Alice: Yes, and I remember you had the Christmas festivities there. Victor was Santa Claus one time and handed out those chocolates that you got every year at Christmas in the great big boxes. They were chocolate creams, and they were good. Once we had a Christmas cantata. I remember it was about "Newsboy Tim" who "had no good house to enter in."

Augusta: I don't remember that, but I do remember that we had programs at Christmas, and I presume at Easter we had something special. And didn't you have a Valentine box? Ninth-grade graduation was always a special event, too. *(See appendix 8—a graduation program handwritten by Augusta inside the cover of a song book.)*

Alice: Oh, yes, we enjoyed all that, too. And I also remember that nice, big school yard we had—at least it seemed big to us then—with the huge oak trees in it at the Orange Park school. When one of the big oaks blew down in a storm, it became the very best playground we kids ever had. I'm sure that now we wouldn't be allowed to climb in it because it would be "dangerous."

Augusta: Did Gladys *(Alice: Gerald's second wife)* speak to you about the principal she has whom she dislikes heartily because he thinks that children don't need to move around in between having to sit at their desks? And she said that he doesn't want them to go out into the yard and play.

Alice: Why?

Augusta: Isn't that ridiculous? He said they might get too disorderly and disturb the ones that are in the other rooms, and I said, "Well, if you go out with them," to Gladys, "you could see to it that they were not too noisy or too wild." And she said she can't do that because her principal doesn't like the teacher telling the children what to play. I was mentioning *Three Deep* and some of those other games that are not at all rough. If the teacher is there and watches a little, of course they really will play better.

She said that wouldn't do because then she wouldn't be letting the children do what they wanted to of their free will. And they're not supposed to run around or make any disturbance of any kind for people who are still in the rooms. I think it is the most ridiculous thing. Gladys says that she knows the children can sit still just so long, and then they have to get up and stir around a little. And she has this principal who seems to think that children should just sit there.

Alice: I know that was always a very important part of our day—getting out, moving around.

Augusta: It is, of course. Naturally, even most grown-up people don't like to sit too long. And when children have been in their desks, maybe for two hours or so, they're ready to get out and move around a little bit—at least play tag or something like that.

Alice: Well, if they don't, there's going to be trouble.

Augusta: I especially mentioned to Gladys that game *Three Deep*, which is certainly not a wild game. I don't know how you could make that very wild. Do you?

Alice: *Some* of them probably could.

Augusta: It's a very good, quiet game. And most children like to play that very much. She said she is not supposed to make them play any certain game. She's supposed to have nothing to do with them out of doors, except when someone gets completely out of bounds. But I guess that doesn't even really ever happen when they're told to be that quiet. She was really very angry with that principal. She said she doesn't like him at all because he thinks that the teachers don't need to move around much, and the children not at all. Sometime when you're with her again, ask her about her principal.

Alice: I will.

Do you remember now the people that you taught with at these various schools? I know in the ones where you were the only teacher, there weren't any others, but I'm trying to remember some of the people, like at Doctors Inlet when you were first there. There's a picture in that album in the den. Apparently Victor was in Mrs. Jenkins' class. Is that right? I mean the first time you were at Doctors Inlet.

Augusta: Yes, Mrs. Jenkins.

Alice: And who else? Do you remember? Weren't there three of you?

Augusta: Some of the others that I can remember—do you remember Mrs. Huntley?

Alice: No, I know of her though. Was that Jack's mother? Or Eva's?

Augusta: You know there were several Huntleys.

Alice: Yes. I don't know who was which. Eleanor Huntley—and then there was—where did you teach with Elva Lee? That was at Doctors Inlet the second time, wasn't it?

Augusta: Yes. I taught with Elva Lee. And who was the primary teacher—who was the one who made trouble? You may remember. She afterward taught at the beach.

Alice: That wasn't Helen Tarr?

Augusta: No, Helen Tarr did teach at Doctors Inlet at one time, but I'm thinking of the one that made so much trouble there.

Alice: I don't know. Maybe that'll come back.

Augusta: And she was Gerald's primary teacher.

Alice: Maybe he'd remember that. In Orange Park, I remember, it was Helen(a) Gabrielson *(Alice: "Miss Helen" to all of her students),* and Clyde Smith Hicks, and you. And at Penney Farms—Grace Thomas? Was she at Penney Farms?

Augusta: I don't know Grace Thomas.

Alice: Was it somebody-else Thomas?

Augusta: Yes, it was another name. Let's see. You're thinking about Grace—

Alice: Oh, I remember! She was Grace Laborda Ford Blatzer Clark.

Augusta: That's the one, with all the former husbands' last names. But that other one I can't think of.

Alice: Alma Thomas!

Augusta: Yes, Alma Thomas.

Alice: And Mrs. Murray from Green Cove drove to Penney Farms with you, didn't she?

Augusta: Yes, she's the one whom I always stopped for in Green Cove and drove out to Penney Farms.

Alice: And then Mrs. Prosser was the principal there. She, also, had a long drive, didn't she?

Augusta: Well, not really—

Alice: No, not any worse than yours, but I mean both of you had long drives.

Augusta: Let me see now. Where did Mrs. Prosser stay? She was with her sister at Doctors Inlet.

Alice: Down on the lake.

Augusta: And of course she died a number of years ago now.

Alice: But she lived a good long time, didn't she?

Augusta: Well, she was really hoping to have a long time after she retired, but she died very soon after she did retire. So she didn't have a long retirement at all. She hoped to live very long because her father had lived very long, and I think he died only very shortly before she did.

Alice: She was the only PhD that you taught with, wasn't she?

Augusta: Yes, I don't think there was any other. I don't remember the man I'm trying to think of who was a principal in Doctors Inlet for a little while. He had no family.

Alice: Not Herndon?

Augusta: It wasn't Herndon. He was one of the teachers, though.

Alice: Mr. Herndon had a wife, though, because when he was running around with Helen Tarr, you thought it was scandalous.

Augusta: Yes. Well, it was!

Alice: His wife was sick, I think?

Augusta: Yes, and he went for summer courses over in Tallahassee at the same time I was there for summer courses. Helen Tarr went there at the same time, and then they were embarrassed because one time all the teachers in summer classes went on some outing, and the two of them were on it, too. Of course, I was the only one there that knew them, and they knew me, and I think they were very much embarrassed that I saw them together. But of course it wasn't any of my business. I didn't even mention it when I got back home. It was really none of my business.

Alice: Well, Henry Wade was one of the others.

Augusta: That's the one I'm trying to think of—Wade!

Alice: F. Henry Wade, wasn't it?

Augusta: He was the principal there at one time.

Alice: At Doctors Inlet?

Augusta: Yes, Doctors Inlet.

Alice: That was the first time around, I guess.

Augusta: Yes.

Alice: I knew him.

Augusta: Did we mention the name "Harrington"?

Alice: No.

Augusta: It seems to me it was Mrs. Harrington that was Gerald's first teacher.

Alice: That's the one! I remember there was trouble with her. They lived in Orange Park, and Gerald's friend, Earl, was her son. Is that right?

Augusta: I guess that's right. I wouldn't be too sure. But I remember that she made a lot of trouble there, too—flirting with various men, and it was ridiculous. You know the grandfather of the Lees was living out that way?

Alice: Cleve Lee?

Augusta: No, Cleve Lee, I think, was just Glen's uncle. This was the grandfather.

Alice: No, I don't know that person.

Augusta: Mrs. Lee's father. He had a little house way up there near Little Black Creek. Do you know anything about that?

Alice: No, I don't.

Augusta: He had a little house out there, and it was ridiculous for her to be friends with him. But she'd go out there to see him, and there were other cases there where she was seen with somebody. And the biggest trouble was in the PTA between her, this teacher, and Mrs. Lee, Glen's mother. Glen's mother disliked this teacher because she was also going after Glen's father.

Alice: Oh, my!

Augusta: And *he* seemed to like *her* pretty well. And Glen's mother naturally didn't like that. But there was all kinds of stuff like that to which I never paid much attention because it was disgusting to have anything like that going on in the community.

Alice: I remember some of the kids you told me about, too.

Augusta: Oh, yes!

Alice: What was that you told me about registration one time? Two of them from one family had a different name or something?

Augusta: Yes, I don't know whether you remember that there was one family where the father was killed, and I think the way he was killed was by one of those old autos you had to crank from the front. When he cranked it, it was in gear, and it ran over him and killed him. Was that Smith?

Alice: Smith is the name that came to my mind.

Augusta: There might have been also various families of Smith—it's such a commonly heard name. But that was the family where there was that mixture of kids. When this man was killed by the car, that woman had the children of at least two men. Now whether she was married to one or the other or both at the time, I don't know. But it was an awfully mixed-up family. That's the one you may remember that I spoke of at the time. And then I would have known more about it than I can remember right now. I do remember that then there were all kinds of conditions there, you know. And nobody really knew what this Mrs. Smith had to live on or where she got any money. So there she had these various children.

Alice: What I remembered, I think, was that at registration, one of them told you, "My name is Smith, but I'm really a Jones," or something like that.

Augusta: Yes, that was it. So his mother must have told him, "Call yourself like the rest of the family, but what you really are is that other."

Alice: And another one that was bragging about a cousin who had "sugar dy-a-bee-teez." He was so proud of that.

Augusta: I remember that. There was a family that lived there near Little Black Creek where the mother died, and there were the father and four sons and one of the sons had diabetes. Now who was that family? One of the boys was always a troublemaker. Jimmy—Jimmy—?

Alice: Mc-something?

Augusta: No, it wasn't anything like that. Victor may remember them because they were living right there near Little Black Creek bridge. I guess their house is still there. Their mother died, and this man was left with four boys, and I had one of them in my class for about two years, and then a younger brother, I think for one year, but I can't now remember the last name. I should because of that Jimmy who was a troublemaker. Howard was one of his brothers. Well, all I can say again is maybe Victor will remember.

Alice: He might.

Augusta: Of course all those things are not very important.

Alice: No, but they're interesting. Kind of local color. I was thinking about the two kids named Callus and Arson, too. There were some interesting names.

Augusta: Some names were funny.

Alice: And you had one boy, I remember, that was seventeen years old in the third grade. Do you remember who that was? (*Victor: Yes, that was "Goat" Manning.*)

Augusta: I remember the fact, but as to any details—

Alice: It really had to be an interesting career—teaching in the country schools.

Augusta: Yes, it was. It was hard work, but I liked it.

That boy was seventeen years old, and then some in the class were only nine or ten.

Alice: I guess that Doctors Inlet was really one of the most interesting places.

Augusta: You know what Victor told me that kind of gave me a shock? I was grouching about people not knowing grammar and diagramming sentences now, and I said again, as I have said many times, there were several years when they weren't taught grammar at all. And then Victor reminded me that I had taught him in the sixth grade, which I did, and in the sixth grade I certainly should have been teaching, and think I did teach, diagramming.

Alice: I'm sure you did.

Augusta: You know I would start them on something very simple, and—

Alice: I remember that.

Augusta: And what he said was that he didn't remember anything about that.

Alice: He just doesn't remember then, because I know you did.

Augusta: So you see, when I blame other teachers for not teaching it, it may be that it's the same thing.

Alice: In many cases, I think that's what it is. Edith Faye *(Alice: A Palm Beach Community College English Department colleague of mine)* told me that one of her former A students who had gone on to a university came back to visit. He sat in on one of her classes in which she was talking about connotation—the connotative meanings of words. After class, he said, "Gosh, Miss Easterling, I sure wish you'd taught that to us when *I* was in your class." She said she looked at him rather sternly and said, "I *did!*" Well, he didn't remember a thing about it. Not a thing! So I think that's probably what happened there, too, with Victor.

Augusta: That happens, I guess, to a good many people.

Alice: It didn't really impress him, I guess. But I know you taught diagramming because I remember seeing it on the board in Orange Park when I came into your classroom after school.

Augusta: Well, you know I asked Victor if he didn't remember how it started very simply, like "Dogs bark," "Most dogs bark," "Most dogs bark fiercely," adding just one part of speech at a time. Just get them to learn one word and where to put it each day. It seems to me that's all right, and of course it should be kept up. I mean not taught all at the same time one day when they'd have to diagram all the parts of speech and where they belong in sentences, then all of a sudden—no more. So I feel that I maybe did teach it.

Alice: You taught it.

Augusta: As thoroughly as I could. And just as Victor has forgotten, many of the others did. Once in a great while now, I come across somebody who does know a little something about diagramming. A very few people— very few. And don't you think that diagramming is so much plainer than when you say, for instance, "An adverb can modify a verb, an adjective, or another adverb"?

Alice: Especially if you don't really understand what verbs, adjectives, and adverbs are. Yes, you can see it right there before you.

Augusta: That doesn't really mean anything to anyone unless you draw a picture of it in a diagram. I think if you do that—go slowly, take one thing one day, something else the next day, and then stick with it—it will work. Let me see—who else recently told me that she did study diagramming? I guess it was Gladys. I must ask her how much she still remembers.

Alice: I do remember it, though. And sometimes I would come over to Doctors Inlet from high school to pick you up in the afternoon when I had used your car, and I can remember that you always did a lot of extra things for the kids that most teachers don't do now. Like having a pretty chalk calendar on the board. I can remember drawing pictures with colored chalk for your calendars a lot of times.

Augusta: Yes, I always tried to have something attractive on the board or on the wall. And especially I'd try to make a lot out of holidays like Christmas, Easter, Flag Day, Valentine's Day, Halloween, and Thanksgiving, because I think that makes a good impression on children.

Something else I did, I think, would help many people who can't do it now—some of them who fail on the examinations they take now—because they don't know how to write. We used to do that in my classroom.

On Friday mornings, I believe, anyway one day in the week, each student had to be ready to tell one interesting news item of that day or maybe the day before, and just in short form. Like "Such and such a volcano erupted last night and killed many people." Something on that order—maybe one sentence. Then after a student had said whatever his or her news item was, all the students would have their pencils and papers ready, and each one would write down one sentence about what that student had said.

And I would send the one that had given it in the first place to the board to write a sentence about it. Of course, that person should know the most about it and should be able to write a good sentence about it. In the first place, it made them realize what a sentence was. They wouldn't write something as a sentence that wasn't a sentence; instead they'd write something that was finished—had subject and predicate and so on.

That was good practice for them, and then, of course, there were always some who misspelled words or left out something.

When that one student had written a sentence on the board with his or her news item, then we'd all take a look at it. If anybody saw anything incorrect, he or she would raise a hand and say what was wrong with it.

That reminds me of a sentence about which someone in the class said, "*Isn't* shouldn't have an apostrophe." Little things like that are funny to remember. *(Alice: For those who don't know why that statement is funny, it is because "isn't" must have an apostrophe to indicate the missing "o" in "not.")*

Alice: But do you realize how far ahead of your time you were? Combining social studies and current events and spelling and grammar? That's what they try to do in a lot of schools now.

Augusta: I always thought that was a very good time to teach them all to write, to even know when they were at the end of a sentence or at the end of a paragraph if it was something longer. But I do remember that every day I had those children, even when I had several grades, all working together and writing something, and you know now where they were trying to give those examinations for high school graduates, some of them were failing because they couldn't write anything and evidently didn't even know when they were at the end of a sentence.

Alice: I had some like those in my English classes.

Augusta: That's awful. But I think that's what every teacher should do—get them to write something. And also to speak correctly. It isn't how much; it's just simply the fact that they do it. If you tell them to write a whole page about something, you may not even have time to look over it.

Augusta: Is there anything else in connection with schools or things about early days?

Alice: Well, one thing more: do you remember how effective the propaganda lessons were for us kids in our schools during the war years?

Augusta: No, I hadn't thought about that.

Alice: We were taught that war was a terrible but beautiful thing, full of heroes and grand patriotism. We sang patriotic songs in school and listened to patriotic songs on "Your Hit Parade," and drew patriotic pictures, and saw patriotic movies in the theaters. In our games, we pretend-killed Nazis and Japanese, as our comic book heroes told us to. And then, of course, there was rationing, which showed us that we were being deprived of the rationed items by the Nazis and the Japanese.

When I was in about the fifth grade, I saved up to buy a little ceramic floral plaque from the dime store to give to you for your birthday. I proudly showed it to my teacher, Mrs. Zelma Hatcher. Remember her? She became angry and scolded me in front of the entire class for not using the money I spent on the plaque to buy "savings stamps" toward the purchase of war bonds. We could buy these stamps in the school, and we were encouraged to do so every week. I was terribly ashamed of myself, as she intended I should be.

We were a very patriotic generation!

Augusta: Yes.

Alice: We were also soundly warned about the evils of alcohol.

On one of our Saturday trips to Green Cove Springs for the week's groceries, we had gone our separate ways—you and Grandma to the A&P store, Gerald to visit his friend Ed Rich, Daddy (I supposed) to either the hardware store or to Roy Davis's shop, and I to the dime store. I was thirteen years old, and my world seemed fine and clean.

When it was time to go home, I left the dime store and walked east on the sidewalk toward the A&P store, looking into the store windows until I reached the middle of the block. That was where the bar was—its door open and its interior dark. I had been taught that alcohol was evil and people who drank it were terrible sinners, so I quickly turned my head to avoid being contaminated by seeing the interior of the dark room and the horrible people in it, but I didn't turn quite quickly enough.

A flash of color caught my eye—Daddy's shirt! He was sitting at the bar holding a glass with foam at the top! How could that be? Didn't he know how terrible the bar was? Should I tell him I had seen him in that disgusting place? Should I tell *you*? I didn't tell anyone about it till now, but something changed in me with that quick sighting of Daddy enjoying an innocent glass of beer.

Augusta: And you kept that a secret all this time! Your daddy would have been so embarrassed if he had known you saw him.

Well, we have talked about this place quite a bit, haven't we? And our chief visitor, Mr. Staub, and the schools and the boats; we've talked about trips to Jacksonville and Auntie's and my accident.

Alice: Oh, yes! We need to add more about the *Alert* because we didn't get all that information in there. You told me about Captain Larson, but we'll have to add the *Alert* to the tape here.

Augusta: Oh, the *Alert*, and I guess what Victor was telling you was that Brian *(Alice: Victor's son.)* went down there?

Alice: He's been down there to look at it, yes.

Augusta: And they never did get the *Alert* up because it had disintegrated too much?

Alice: He said there's only a little bit of it sticking up above the mud now, anyway. The rest of it is covered by silt.

Augusta: And of course nobody ever will know, I guess, although there may be somebody living who knows all about it—I mean what happened to him and what happened to the money that was there. There was a little cabin where the captain steered, and there he had a little desk with a drawer where he kept the orders he was to fill in Jacksonville. What money he had was in there.

Now what happened to all that? Of course it might have gone down and still be in the mud, but they looked for quite a while, and nobody could find anything.

Alice: Do you remember about when that was?

Augusta: Let's see. I think Victor remembers that.

Alice: He probably does. (*Victor: Probably about 1920.*)

Augusta. I'll tell you what I was wondering—if that could have been the one that had stopped at our neighbor's place. (*Alice: Victor identifies her as Mrs. Willis.*) Now Victor may know her name. But that woman who lived next door then was not an admirable character. She would have men stop over there. Evidently it was all supposed to be business, you know—stuff that they were bringing her or taking somewhere for her. But she had them over there as visitors sometimes quite a while, and it was—well, not exactly a joke on her—but in a way it was. When we went to the post office for the mail, if there was any mail for her, we'd bring it, and somebody would take it over to her.

One year, when I was away teaching, your dad was here by himself, and Mrs. Willis was over there. So when I was gone, of course, your dad still went over to Rideout Post Office for the mail, and the paper came that way, too. Then when there was any mail that had come for Mrs. Willis, he'd take it over there to her.

Now, that's all we know. But when I came home, your father was completely disgusted with Mrs. Willis. He wouldn't go over there. He didn't even want us to have anything to do with her. So we knew what she had been trying to do. And he wouldn't bring her mail to her anymore. If there was anything to take to her, some of the rest of us had to do it.

And then she wrote to him. It came in our mail—a letter or a card or whatever it was from her to your father—and he wouldn't even open it. He took it right on back the next time he had a chance to go to Rideout, and he told Mr. Frisbee, the postmaster, to give it to Mrs. Willis and to tell her it was returned as "not wanted." And I think that was the end of that. She found out then that she couldn't bother him anymore.

Alice: He was not interested.

Augusta: He never said anything, really. But we could just tell by his way with the letter she had sent him, which he didn't want, and then he would never go over there again and indicated that she was not to come here. She soon moved away. But I just thought that was awful, because we had tried to be good neighbors to her, and just as soon as your father was alone, here she came. So we don't know exactly what happened with the *Alert* and all that. I do remember something about some boat having stopped at Mrs. Willis's place, and I think it was the one that then turned over up there. The idea just came up in general that he might have been drunk because he knew the Creek so well that there really wasn't any reason why he should have run ashore or too near shore and tipped over and then fallen in and not been able to get out.

The Alert

Alice: That does seem strange.

Augusta: And all the money gone. Now there were two or three passengers— men, I think, all of them—but they said they knew nothing. There might have been more. I don't think any of them drowned, but they couldn't tell about anything. Naturally, if any one of them had taken the money, he wouldn't tell, and now we may never know.

Augusta, c. 1905

Marguerite's graduation from Stetson University, 1914

Bathing costumes, 1911

Earl sailed on the Astral around Cape Horn.

One-room schoolhouse and students, possibly Highland School

Augusta among the palmettos

Augusta with kitten

Jane Thorp, honoring son Earl, who served in World War I, 1918

Marguerite, swimming instructor, Bristol, Virginia, 1920s

Marie and Alice Marie hunting Easter eggs, c. 1935

G. W. Thorp's stone-cutting invention, courtesy Della Shafer

Gerald (left)—US Marine Corps; Victor (right)—US Navy, World War II

Left to right, Gerald, US Marie Corps, Augusta, Earl, Victor, US Navy, c. 1946

Victor—World War II; Earl—World War I

Left to right, Geneta Frisbee, Shirley Negrich, Verla Fountain, Alice Marie Thorp, Adelaide Simmons, Nannie May Saunders. Part of CHS class of 1949. In background: Martha Rogers, Senior Sponsor, History, Music.

Alice Marie and Augusta, Daytona Beach, 1948

CHAPTER 3

Life in Rural Northeast Florida, Early and Mid-1900s—Two Wars and the Great Depression

I can only imagine how the people who lived in the Clay County, Black Creek area of North Florida must have felt in the spring of 1911 when the "foreigners" moved in. Not only were the Pflugs "foreigners" but the two elders, Max and Marie, spoke with German accents.

Then those foreigners put a fence around their own thirty acres to mark their property and to keep out the neighbors' stock. Florida, at that time, was "open range" country, which meant that the owners of livestock (cattle, hogs, goats, etc.) were not required to fence in their animals, and the people to whose land the animals had open access could do nothing about it except to fence their own property to keep the animals out.

Such an effort, however, inevitably resulted in cut fences when the owners of stock wanted their animals to have more grazing range. A fence also made it inconvenient for the locals to walk across the property when they wanted to take shortcuts to the houses of friends or relatives. So, there were three strikes against the Pflugs at the very start: they were foreigners, they talked funny, and they put up a fence.

It was not until 1950 that Florida enacted a law that required owners to fence in their stock in order to keep the animals off the roads and out of unfenced neighboring properties. In the meantime, the natives made the Pflugs' property available to all people and grazing animals by simply cutting the Pflugs' fence.

I do not know what resistance the elder Thorps, George and Jane, might have faced, if any, when they arrived five years later, but they decided, after only a few years, to return to Kansas. I do not know whether that was due in any part to unfriendliness, or rather due to the pleas they received from friends in Kansas for them to return to Conway Springs, where George could again open his blacksmith shop. I do know that the Pflugs' fence was cut as soon as it was installed and required repair and replacement many times. The effort of repair was viewed as hopeless when, finally, entire sections of the fence disappeared. This battle of wills went on for some time and could not have been pleasant.

Additionally, the farmers around them grew paying crops, but the Pflugs were mainly unsuccessful at farming.

The attractive Pflug daughters, Augusta and Marguerite, were well educated, both soon working as teachers, Augusta in the immediate area and Marguerite at Virginia Intermont College in Bristol, Virginia. That must have been shocking to neighbors who generally didn't think women needed to be educated.

When the local lads came calling, the Pflug daughters politely greeted them and then invited them for a walk—to the gate at the end of their driveway, where they would open the gate, thank the lads for coming, close the gate, and return to the house. That was surely unacceptable behavior by local standards.

Augusta at gate

If there was animosity, however, it must have faded over time. When Augusta taught in the little Pine Grove one-room school, she was well liked by the students. Many of those students still remembered and respected her sixty years later when they gathered around her at her sister's funeral in Oakland Cemetery in 1972. My brothers and I encountered no resentment that I am aware of in school. Of course, during World War II, I did not mention to my classmates that my mother and grandmother spoke German at home, and that although my grandmother could speak English quite well, albeit with a heavy accent, she missed having others with whom to speak her native language. Nor did I tell anyone that there were swastikas painted around the ceiling of my bedroom. They were not Nazi swastikas; they were Indian good fortune symbols that my father, part Cherokee, had painted there, but I doubt our neighbors and schoolmates would have made the distinction. Victor and Gerald were respected for serving in the navy and marine corps, respectively, during World War II. So far as I know, there was no significant disapproval of our half-German–part-Native-American family by the time I would have been aware of it during my schooldays.

The Pflugs' lifestyle after they moved to Florida changed significantly from that to which they had been accustomed. They had been living in large towns in Germany, Austria, and the United States where they had servants, electric or gas lighting, indoor bathrooms with running water, a social life for the parents, and many friends close by for the children. They had crossed the Atlantic several times, according to my grandfather's business needs. Their daughters, Augusta and Marguerite, had attended excellent schools in Switzerland, Germany, and the United States, and had started college in New Jersey. Their brother, Oscar, had attended military schools because his father thought a strict, military training was essential for boys.

After their move to Black Creek in rural North Florida in 1911, things changed. Max, Marie, and Augusta found themselves miles from any town, distant from all their friends, without servants, without electricity or gas lighting, and without running water and indoor bathrooms. It must have taken some getting used to. They apparently adjusted to the changes well, however, since I never heard complaints from my mother in later years concerning that time.

Winter picnic—Max and Marie waiting for the train to Jacksonville

Marguerite visited Florida only on summer breaks and at Christmastime. Oscar was in business in New York and overseas and also enjoyed only brief visits until his untimely death in 1929. Augusta, as the elder daughter, remained in the new home as helper and later caregiver for her parents.

It must have been difficult for my mother and grandmother to take on the full responsibility of managing the home and property when Max died in 1919, only eight years into his retirement. His death left the two women alone until Augusta married Earl Thorp a year later.

The Depression nearly wiped out the money the Pflug family still had in the local bank. Maintenance of the home and property fell to what little was left in the bank and to what Augusta could earn teaching and Earl could earn at various jobs, such as blacksmith work, auto repairs, and construction.

It is so easy to look back at those years from today's perspective and wonder how we managed to live contentedly without the many conveniences we take for granted today. The answer is simple. We just did, and we didn't know we were inconvenienced because that was simply the way things were. I have been asked what it was like living without running water, electricity, and the entertainment choices families have today. What did we do without paved roads? Did we have enough food during the Depression?

How did we celebrate holidays? And what in the world did we do for medical care, living so far from town?

Come back with me to rural Northeast Florida in the first half of the twentieth century, to the large, white frame house near Black Creek.

This is what I remember.

No running water?

Our water was drawn by a pitcher pump through a pipe placed in a well dug deep enough to reach the aquifer. The water was cold and always tasted good, except for the one brief, unfortunate, dead-snake episode mentioned earlier.

White-enameled water buckets, refilled whenever necessary during the day, were carried from the well, about one hundred feet south of the house, and kept on a small table in the kitchen.

We had two buckets. One was on the right side of the table for drinking water, with a dipper made by my father, Earl, to fill our glasses. (We would *never* think of drinking from the dipper, itself.) The second bucket on the left side of the table was used for washing our hands and brushing our teeth, using a basin that stood on another table across from the water bucket table.

Soiled water from the basin was poured into a "slop bucket" on the floor, to be emptied on plants or trees when it was full. Although the contents of both water buckets came from the same source, it was not allowed that we should dip a drink from the "washing water" bucket or waste the "drinking water" bucket contents on hand-washing or dishwashing.

When the enamel on a bucket became chipped, the bucket was retired and a new bucket was purchased and became the new drinking water bucket. The damaged bucket was demoted accordingly to wash water bucket or slop bucket.

On hot summer afternoons, one of us would be sent to fetch a bucket of freshly pumped, cold drinking water. It was colder and more refreshing than any other drink could possibly be.

For washing dishes, we had a larger table, in front of the window in the west wall of the kitchen, on which we used two large basins—one with hot water to wash dishes and utensils and another to rinse them. Once they were washed, we placed the dishes and utensils into a drying rack until they were dried with clean kitchen towels. The hot water was created by combining water from the washing water bucket with water boiled on the stove. The same table served for food preparation.

On bath nights in the earliest years, we used a large, round, galvanized metal tub, filled with cold water from the well, warmed by water that we boiled on the kerosene stove in a very large copper kettle that my father made. In later years, we would have a rectangular bathtub made of rubberized, waterproof canvas material on a wooden frame that could be folded for storage, rather like a wooden cot could be folded. We took our baths in the kitchen because it was a small room and could be more easily heated by a kerosene heater on cold nights, and because that's where the stove was to boil the water. On nonbath nights, we took sponge baths, using the basin.

The most practical bathing events, however, took place in the hot summer months. Every afternoon in summer, barring seriously stormy days, we walked down to our dock on Black Creek in our bathing suits, carrying our washcloths, soap, and shampoo. The brand of soap was very important. Only Ivory soap, living up to its famous motto "It floats!" was practical to use for bathing on the steps of our dock on the south side of the Creek. If we accidentally dropped the soap into the Creek, it would not sink, and we could rescue it before it drifted away.

There were no other houses along our part of the Creek bank, so we had relative privacy, disturbed only by small boats occasionally passing by and, rarely, large ones. Then we could modestly pretend that we were just sitting and resting from vigorous swimming, not actually taking baths, even though we had to do so modestly with our bathing suits on. That resulted in some contortions for a full-body wash, but the Creek's naturally soft water was excellent for cleanliness and for freshly shampooed, shiny hair. Rinsing required only diving in and swimming about.

My father, who preferred not to bathe in the Creek, had made himself a long, galvanized metal bathtub, held upright by a strong wooden frame, which he kept at his workshop behind a thicket of large, moss-hung oak trees. He carried water early in the day to fill his tub and then bathed later in the day after several hours of direct solar heat provided a warm, comfortable bath, secluded from curious eyes by the oaks and their moss.

No running water meant no "facilities." We supplied that lack by having chamber pots under or beside each bed. These were emptied and rinsed far into the woods every morning, each one the responsibility of its user. Only very small children and persons afflicted with sickness were immune to the morning ritual.

Of course, there was also an outhouse to provide for such needs. It was downhill, also about one hundred feet from the house but far northwest from the well. It was a hardy, brave soul, however, who ventured out on a cold, dark winter night to use it. Even warm nights did not bring the outhouse many visitors, because of the inconvenience and sometimes the concern of having only the light from our flashlights to guide us. The path was frequently used by wild animals and snakes, and surrounded by clouds of mosquitoes in summer. Sometimes animals or snakes invaded the outhouse, too, and mosquitoes certainly did. We were, therefore, not resentful of having to empty our own chamber pots each morning.

Many years before, the wooden outhouse structure had been dragged behind the family's Model T Ford from a neighbor's property to its present location behind the luxuriant screen of two very large bamboo clumps. Thus a trip down that way was referred to as "going to the Bamboo," a euphemism that might amuse but not offend visitors.

Our outhouse was not furnished as other outhouses usually were. There was no dry corncob or *Sears, Roebuck* catalog, such as cartoons usually portrayed. There was a roll of real toilet tissue, and it was the responsibility of the person who depleted the roll to deliver another immediately to the Bamboo, often setting off the common disagreement among family members about whether the paper should pull from over or under the roll.

Laundry was done next to the pump in two large, round, galvanized tubs, one for washing and one for rinsing, and hung on wire clotheslines with spring clip clothespins to dry. (Are you noticing the importance of galvanized metal? That was the only strong metal available to us that was rust resistant.) This gave the benefit of sunlight, which both sterilized and bleached the laundry with the assistance of a little "bluing," the only additive to Oxydol or Ivory Flakes considered necessary to make the white things look whiter.

Elmer on clothes pole

Laundry that should not be bleached by the sun was hung on a line shaded by trees, and, yes, it was occasionally soiled by birds sitting in those trees. Elmer, our black and white cat, sitting on the top of one of the posts that supported the clotheslines, kept us company while we were toiling over the laundry.

There was no washing machine with a wringer, so all of the laundry, including the sheets and towels, was wrung out by hand. Often two of us made a game of it by taking opposite ends of a sheet and twisting as hard as we could until the "loser" could not twist anymore. My father fashioned a very effective copper device that looked like a big metal funnel with air holes in it on a long wooden handle, with which the laundry could be agitated more aggressively than by hand in the tub with soap and water.

No scent additives, such as those that would be available in later years to freshen the wash, could possibly match the clean, happy scent of laundry dried on the clothesline by the sun and a fresh breeze. We changed the linens on our beds once a week, usually on Sunday, and it was pure sensuous luxury to sleep on and under those freshly washed, clean-smelling, sun-and-wind-dried percale sheets.

For extremely dirty laundry, we had a large, round, black cast iron pot, also known as a "witch's pot" for obvious reasons, with space enough below it to build a wood fire that would boil very dirty laundry to remove the soil. That seldom needed to be used, however.

The first modern washing machine did not arrive at our house until the 1950s. It was a front loader that would live on the south porch of the house and provide great entertainment for Mac, the family dog, by "walking" noisily across the uneven porch boards when it was in use.

No electricity?

Our nighttime illumination was provided by several kerosene lamps—some portable, some attached to the wall, and one hanging from the ceiling. Ordinary kerosene lamps provided a rather dim light for schoolwork or reading or cooking and baking at night, but one of our lamps, an Aladdin kerosene lamp with a "mantle" rather than the usual wick, provided almost as much light as a 100-watt bulb. That lamp hung over the dining room table because that was our default spot for doing homework, reading, eating, sewing, and playing games at night.

We lit the portable kerosene lamps in our bedrooms for dressing, undressing, and late reading.

We also kept flashlights by our beds for any light needed during the night.

We children learned quite early how to light and extinguish our lamps and were necessarily responsible with our use of matches and not wasteful of the flashlights' batteries.

The glass lamp chimneys needed daily cleaning to remove smoke from their inner surfaces. The Aladdin lamp required great care in lighting, extinguishing, and cleaning because of the fragility of its mantle, which could crumble at a touch, so we always needed at least one spare mantle on hand.

Despite Chamber of Commerce claims to the contrary, North Florida can often be quite cold in the wintertime. That necessitated augmentation for the fireplace, which was the only built-in heat in the house. Since there was no electricity, a kerosene heater was the only (relatively) safe choice, and it was quite effective if one remained in a room with the burning heater and kept the windows closed.

We knew that there were enough gaps under and around the doors and windows and through the keyholes to avoid the danger of oxygen depletion. Barring an occasional, accidental flare-up when fuel spilled out or the heater fell over or chose to malfunction, our kerosene heater was an excellent provider of warmth, its major limitation being that a person could warm only one side at a time.

With no electricity in the kitchen, our kerosene stove provided a fairly reliable source of heat for cooking and baking. The stove had two cylindrical burners for pots and pans and another burner for an eye-level oven. Since the heat was controlled by the adjustment of the round wicks that soaked up the kerosene, gravity-fed to each burner from the tank next to them, we learned to gauge the height and color of the flame for the proper adjustments, and we learned the importance of keeping the wicks trimmed evenly.

The oven on our kerosene stove had a thermometer in its door so that we could bake with nearly exact heat by adjusting the flame below the oven. A blue flame was desirable and produced less smoke than a yellow flame, and an uneven flame meant the wick had not been properly trimmed.

Many other families cooked on woodstoves that also required careful adjustments and the chopping or sawing, carrying, and storing of wood to supply the stoves. We considered ourselves fortunate to have our fine, modern, green kerosene stove with its surprisingly accurate oven.

Without electricity for a refrigerator, we kept only nonperishable foods in the screened "food safe," a cabinet that sat in the kitchen with each leg centered in a small, shallow, metal tray filled with kerosene to discourage ants and roaches from climbing up to get at the food. (I am sure that only great care saved us from going up in smoke during these years.)

We tried to cook only what was necessary for each meal, and we seldom had leftovers, but when we did, they were usually eaten at the next meal.

In cold weather, we could store fresh milk and meat for a day or so in the small room next to the kitchen because that room remained cold for several days after a cold front moved through. We used canned milk instead of fresh milk and margarine instead of butter, because they would keep longer, and we had fresh meat and poultry only on Sundays and holidays. The margarine was white when we bought it, but the package contained a dye pack of yellow color to mix in, so that it would be more appealing and look more like butter.

The kerosene stove also heated flat irons for ironing clothes and my grandmother's marcelling iron for waving her hair.

No entertainment?

TVs, computers, iPads, multiplex cinemas, Nintendos, video games, and other such sources of entertainment would not be invented for many decades, so you well might wonder what we did for entertainment. For one thing, we could go to movies in either of the two theaters in Green Cove Springs. For much less than a dollar, we could see a fairly current, full-length movie, a newsreel, a cartoon, and often a cliffhanger "short," to be continued the following week.

But there was entertainment outdoors, also. Every year, our parents had the pecan grove plowed or disked in early summer to destroy the weeds, and that was fun because we could watch the neighbor's horse at work pulling the plow and turning over the soil as his owner guided the plow or disk to make rows that were absolutely straight.

After the work was done, we waited eagerly for the first hard summer rain to wash the sand away from arrowheads and other Indian relics that had been buried deep by time but were brought to the surface when the hard rain packed down the loose dirt around each relic, leaving it standing on its own pillar of loose sand. Some of the arrowheads and other relics were in excellent condition, and they served to remind us that the banks of the Creek were once the site of fierce battles between the government and the Indians in the 1800s and earlier, and among competing tribes, also. Now they are a metaphorical battleground for the people who want to save the beautiful Creek and its environs and the ones who wish only to enjoy it for themselves, without concern for its survival. *(Alice: Years later, it was heartbreaking to learn that the arrowheads and other relics had been unintentionally thrown away, mistaken for rocks and trash.)*

As he was plowing or disking, the neighbor kept a watch for snakes. If he saw one, he seized it by its tail, whirled it like a whip, and snapped its head off. So far as we were concerned, this was really bad because he did it whether it was a "good" snake or a "bad" snake. And we really considered it a bad thing to do, in general. It was entertaining only for the plowman. Our entertainment lay in finding the relics and in imagining their histories.

We also looked forward eagerly to our aunt's visits at Christmas time when she always took my brothers and me to Jacksonville to see a newly released film, such as *A Christmas Carol*, still in black and white, of course (1938), and *The Wizard of Oz* (1939), our first experience with the magic of Technicolor.

Weekdays, when we arrived home from school, we listened to radio programs, such as *Latitude Zero*, *The Shadow*, and *Little Orphan Annie*, and on weekend nights we listened to *Jack Benny*, *Fred Allen*, *Fibber McGee and Molly*, *Bob Hope*, the *Hit Parade*, the *Great Gildersleeve*, the *Grand Ole Opry*, the *Voice of Firestone*, and many more, but we had to be very careful not to use up the charge in the huge B battery that the radio required, and I discovered that I could very briefly recharge the battery by brushing my hair vigorously next to the radio on a cold, dry, winter night.

My mother often listened to *Vic and Sade* or soap operas on summer afternoons when she was ironing clothes. Daily required listening included the news each evening, as reported by H. V. Kaltenborn, Lowell Thomas, Edward R. Murrow, and other commentators. We could not even begin to imagine that someday in the future we would be able to find those same radio programs on something called the Internet, or even imagine that such a thing as the Internet could exist. But there were many other things that entertained us in these early days.

A form of auditory entertainment was the spring-wound Victrola that sat on a small table in the parlor. My grandfather had bought it years before, especially to listen to recordings of Enrico Caruso, the famous tenor of the early 1900s, but by the time my brothers and I listened to it, many newer records had joined the collection, mostly classical or semiclassical, with some popular music.

"HIS MASTER'S VOICE"

This trademark and the trademarked word "Victrola" identify all our products. Look under the lid! Look on the label!

VICTOR TALKING MACHINE CO., Camden, N. J.

Victor Talking Machine Company Logo (1921)

During World War II, it was sometimes difficult to find the replaceable steel needles that the Victrola required, so Gerald improvised with cactus thorns. The illustration above is the iconic image of the Victrola with its optimistic motto, "His Master's Voice." The model shown is much like the Victrola we had, only ours had an internal horn. The handle on the side would wind up the spring, and we could adjust the speed, if we wished to do so, with a lever below the turntable. Twin doors opened on the front to allow the sound to come out and to allow us to control the volume.

Books—lots of books! There was always something to read on the shelves in our parlor. The mix was eclectic, and the dates of publication ranged from pre-1900 to whatever the year might be when we searched. If all else failed and our chores and homework were done, there was always a book that wanted reading.

Over the years, there were also current copies of *National Geographic*, *Nature* magazine, *Life* magazine, *Seventeen*, the *Saturday Evening Post*, *Liberty* magazine, *Parents* magazine, *Boys' Life*, *Child Life*, and the *Reader's Digest*. All of them had something interesting to tell us, no matter what our ages might be. All this entertaining reading had the added benefit of making school easy for me.

Walks and explorations in the woods provided both physical and visual entertainment. In fall, we saw autumn leaves on the maples, sweet gums, oaks, and sumac, red berries on dogwood trees, wild purple asters, and occasionally deer or foxes or wild turkeys, or we might very rarely hear the chilling cry of a panther.

In winter, the native hollies were glorious, and the wind blew small whitecaps on the Creek on cold, windy days. On still winter days, the remaining autumn leaves reflected from the dark, calm waters of the Creek.

In spring, there were redbuds, dogwoods, wild plums, violets, irises, wild azaleas, new spring-green leaves, various lilies in moist woodlands, and numerous less flamboyant wildflowers, many with their own beautiful visiting hummingbirds and butterflies.

Alice Marie and Augusta's dogwood trees

In early summer, the magnolia and sweet bay blossoms perfumed the heavy air ahead of the torrential summer thunderstorms.

Twice a year—autumn and late winter—we heard and saw large flocks of migrating robins and waxwings. All year around, we saw ibises, herons, egrets, alligators, frogs, and snakes along the Creek. There was always something to see, hear, enjoy, and wonder about.

Perhaps I should explain here why "Creek" is usually used alone and capitalized in this account. Black Creek is such an important part of our lives that we refer to it as the "Creek," as if there were no other creeks around. There are, but any others that are occasionally referred to must have their first names provided in a formal manner, such as Bradley's Creek, Peter's Creek, Governor's Creek, and Little Black Creek, but Black Creek is a dear and personal friend.

Exploring the Creek and its tributaries in our rowboat helped to pass many summer hours, as did playing on the clean, white beach at low tide next to our dock. Each summer we saw enormous, slippery, black tadpoles in calmer areas of the Creek, and sometimes manatees visited our part of the Creek and stayed briefly in a cove across the Creek and west of our dock.

Augusta "Evinruding" with new outboard motor

Frequently, my brothers and I heard the distant, deep rumble of diesel engines from beyond the eastern bend of the Creek, and we would run down to our dock as fast as we could to see one of the fancy yachts that occasionally came up the Creek from the Saint Johns River. The excitement escalated when the passengers sitting on the decks, looking relaxed and very worldly, deigned to notice us and waved to us. That created a brief magical connection to a glamorous world far from our humble country setting—the kind of world we had seen in *Life* magazine.

Sugarcane grinding on a cold winter day in the neighborhood

At night, we often played games—Checkers, Dominoes, Authors, and other games—or just talked or read. Sometimes there were affairs at school to attend—a visiting performer, a play, a lecture, a picnic, a meeting, a concert, a rehearsal, or a party. Such affairs were, of course, limited for us by the inconvenience of travel over the unpaved roads and the ferry.

During the daytime, there were always dogs and cats, each with a special personality, to enjoy, play with, and walk with. And there were toys, some homemade, some store-bought, and many improvised. I especially remember a full set of building blocks my father made for me from oak and cedar scraps from his workshop.

Another source of entertainment for us was, perhaps surprisingly, the post office. We waited eagerly for packages containing items we had ordered from *Sears, Roebuck, Montgomery Ward, Johnson-Smith Company,* and other mail order sources. Many of our items of clothing and often our shoes would come to us by mail. We sent penciled outlines of our feet with our order blanks, and someone at *Sears, Roebuck* matched them to the proper size of the shoes we had chosen from the catalog.

Other clothing and shoes were bought in Jacksonville at Cohen's or other department stores, but the store purchase could not equal the anticipation of the arrival of a package by mail. We welcomed handwritten letters and cards from family members and friends from throughout the United States and from overseas. And, of course, the post office brought our magazines, newspapers, and more books from friends and relatives or a book club.

For as long as I can remember, our post office was a tiny shack in Russell by the railroad tracks. The train bringing the mail didn't even stop at Russell unless there was a passenger to step off, but it did slow down as it passed by. The postmaster hung the outgoing mail bag on an arm attached to a train-high metal pole installed beside the tracks for a railroad employee to reach out and grab, and the same employee threw out our incoming mail in a canvas bag beside the tracks for our postman to pick up, making us fear for fragile packages. For a while, our postmaster, Morgan Williams, was also our school bus driver and a good friend to all of us who rode on his bus.

My brothers and I had fun attending summer camps. Our aunt sent Victor and Gerald to Camp Echockotee, a Boy Scout camp on Doctors Lake in Orange Park, and Gerald and I attended Virginia Intermont Ranch Camp for several years, near Bristol, Virginia, where our aunt was camp director. I cannot speak for my brothers' experiences in the Boy Scout camp, but I loved the ranch camp experience and especially the horses. After my initiation into horseback riding at V.I. Ranch Camp, I occasionally borrowed our neighbors' plow horse, Fly, to ride bareback around the countryside.

There were monthly trips to Jacksonville for shopping that could not be done in Green Cove Springs. Jacksonville was an exciting change of scene and seemed a huge city to us children. Usually we parked the car in Ortega, a suburb some distance from the center of town. Then we took a bus into the city.

Max and Marie at the railroad bridge

One of our favorite things in Cohen's Department Store was to watch the entire process of doughnuts being mixed, formed, and fried, all in one big, glass-covered machine. My mother always bought us a small bag of nonpareils in Cohen's to enjoy as we walked around.

We also liked to look at our feet on the X-ray device in Cohen's shoe department. It looked rather like a tall scale that we stood on to look through eyepieces aimed at the bones in our feet. No one seemed to know or care that it was a potentially dangerous device, but in a few years, the device was gone. As an article to be written several years later would point out, the gravest danger was to the shoe department clerks who used it on their customers many times during a day.

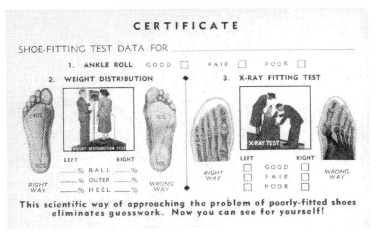

Shoe-fitting certificate

And that reminds me of another source of entertainment that would be considered horrifying in later years. When a thermometer broke, we played with the mercury, watching it roll around in our hands. It looked and behaved like nothing else in our familiar world of solids, liquids, and gases.

Finally, an exciting entertainment for us children was riding to special places in our parents' cars or our aunt's car. My mother recorded the following under *"Baby's First Outing (and others)"* in Gerald's baby book, a small book in which important events in each baby's life were recorded: *"June 19, 1928—St. Augustine (via new Shands Bridge)—Hastings—Palatka, about 130 miles."*

That trip was probably in my aunt's car, since she usually came to visit early in the summer and often had a new car.

A few of the other, later trips my mother included in Gerald's book were: *"Nov. 1932—to Bristol, Va. by bus with Grandma." "Christmas 1932—Round trip from and to Virginia in Auntie's car." "Christmas 1933—Trip to South Fla."*

Even when my brothers and I grew older, a trip of more than the distance to Green Cove Springs or Jacksonville was an entertaining event. I particularly remember special trips to Daytona Beach, Marineland, and Silver Springs. We especially enjoyed riding to Saint Augustine, walking and picnicking on the beach, seeing the fort, and exploring the historic town.

Usually, during the 1940s when Victor came home on leave from the navy, he took us on special trips like the ones above. I don't believe we children ever kicked the back of the front seat and whined, "Are we there yet?" And by parental decree, we did not throw trash out of the windows of the car.

No paved road?

We had no paved road yet to reach the highways to Jacksonville and Green Cove Springs, only a sandy, graded road. We could get to Jacksonville in the shortest time by crossing the Creek on the hand-pulled ferry not far from our house. Problems resulted with that route, however; when the Creek flooded, hyacinths covered the Creek entirely, the cable broke, or some damage to the ferry itself occurred.

Flooded Creek

It usually took us forty-five minutes to an hour to reach Jacksonville by car, but when my grandmother, grandfather, and mother made trips to Jacksonville in the early 1900s, they usually boarded a passenger boat from their dock on the Creek. That boat took them to the mouth of the Creek where it flowed into the Saint Johns River (the longest river in Florida and one of the few in the United States that flow north) and then north to Jacksonville. The trip took about four hours, one way.

Another way for them to get to Jacksonville was to catch a train at the railroad bridge across the Creek, about two miles away by boat or canoe. Of course it was necessary to flag down the train to indicate that passengers wished to board.

A trip to Jacksonville by horse and buggy was not practical unless the traveler planned to spend the night in town. After my grandfather purchased his Model T Ford, family members could get to Jacksonville or Green Cove Springs more quickly in good weather. In bad weather, trips were often ordeals through deep sand in dry weather or slick clay in wet weather.

We had two sand roads out to the main graded road from our property. One we called the "Cross-lay" because our father laid small sections of logs across it to make it usually passable in wet weather when it became muddy. The other, longer road was called the "Detour" because it was on higher ground so that we could get out, even when very heavy rains made the Cross-lay impassable. Sometimes even in the 1940s, in unusually wet conditions we could not leave our property by car because of the flooding in the woods between our house and the graded road.

Ferryman on flooded road

When I began the first grade in 1937, my mother drove my brothers and me to school in Orange Park where she was the principal. We left very early in the morning to make the trip across the Creek on the ferry and over about ten miles of road, partly paved, to reach the school.

Orange Park School

159

Much of the road was east-west, so that my mother faced the morning and late afternoon sun directly as she drove. She attributed her later eye problem (macular degeneration) at least partially to that.

When my mother left Orange Park School to teach at Penney Farms Elementary School in 1940, she had a longer trip each day. My brothers and I then attended Clay County Elementary, Junior High, and High schools, all at the same location in Green Cove Springs.

My older brother, Victor, drove us to our school, and then my mother drove the additional six or seven miles to Penney Farms. After Victor graduated, Gerald and I rode an ancient, rattle-y bus to school, except for the times when Gerald drove us in our father's car while Earl was away, working in Hawaii.

Clay High School bus

After Gerald graduated, I still rode the school bus; only in 1946, a fine, new bus had finally been provided for our route.

It seemed a great adventure to us when one of the bridges on the road to Highway 17 broke under the weight of an overloaded pulp wood truck. Then, for a week or more, we parked the bus on our side of the bridge, walked through the woods over to the railroad tracks, and crossed the little creek on the railroad bridge on foot, after which we boarded another bus that delivered us to school.

In the late 1940s, when my mother taught at Doctors Inlet School, I earned my driver's license. I would sometimes take her to her school and then drive on to Clay High School in the morning, reversing my trip at the end of the day.

In spite of all the traveling, I liked school, and I was pleased when I saw the sure signs that it was school time at the end of summer, when the "school berries" ("French mulberries" or "beauty berries") turned purple and the goldenrod bloomed.

What did you have to eat in the difficult times?

The difficult times were called the Great Depression, which lasted approximately ten years, from 1929 to 1939. We could buy groceries on credit and pay over a period of time, but that was not a practice to be abused, and my parents were very careful with their spending.

One spring and summer, our south yard was filled with a healthful crop of black-eyed peas that supplemented many meals. In summer, we sometimes grew tomatoes. In late summer, there were wild grapes, and one year my father made wine from them, but I was not allowed to taste it.

The pecans ripened late in fall, and some years we had fairly good crops of them, at least enough for us to crack and use for our mother's special Thanksgiving and Christmas baking. The pecan-cracking became an annual tradition. Gerald and I argued over which of us got to use the "good" nutcracker, an antique that functioned extremely well.

Also in autumn, the pears ripened on our trees, and my grandmother or mother preserved them in large Mason jars for desserts like *apfelkuchen* (a sort of pie with sweet crust, topped with apples and meringue), or we often ate them right off the tree.

Some local families gave us vegetables, or a pork shoulder, or whatever they wished to share as thanks for letting their children ride with us to school.

During the war years, we had a few chickens that supplied us with eggs and, inevitably, a solemn dinner when they no longer produced.

Very seldom did we eat fish from the Creek, and when many other foods were rationed during the war years, we moderated their use or stopped using them entirely.

Meals began with an impatient but requisite blessing: "WethanktheeLordfortheseandallotherblessingsamen." Thus we wasted little time getting to the food.

A typical weekday supper was *frikadellen*, navy beans, and boiled potatoes. The fried frikadellen patties made from canned corned beef mixed with bread and onions were one example of many German recipes revised to suit the ingredients that were available in wartime Florida. A typical Sunday meal consisted of well-cooked round steak, mashed potatoes, and a vegetable, and ended with a homemade pie, cake, or cookies.

What did you do to celebrate birthdays and holidays?

Birthday celebrations were not elaborate. Usually there were simple, necessarily inexpensive presents. I remember asking for and happily receiving notebook paper for school, pencils with No. 2 lead, crayons, clothing, books, but nothing expensive or impractical. We seldom had birthday cakes—I don't know why. Probably no one had time to make cakes, but my father sometimes made me a birthday pumpkin pie, my favorite pie. For our parents' and grandmother's birthdays, we picked wildflowers for bouquets, bought a small gift, if we could, and that was about it, because we children had no more than a few pennies, nickels, or dimes.

For Arbor Day, we usually planted a tree at school or at home, or both.

For Valentine's Day, in our classrooms we had elaborately decorated valentine boxes into which we put valentines for our friends, and we had a party during which the valentines were passed out. The ceremony of passing out valentines would later be considered unkind to the children who received few or no valentines from their classmates. My brothers and I gave our mother a box of candy, when we could.

For Easter, we usually attended the sunrise service by the river in Green Cove Springs at the Spring Park. Then we had Easter egg hunts at home, and we received our Easter baskets containing *lots* of chocolate.

For Memorial Day, we hung our flag on the front porch.

For the Fourth of July, we usually had a bonfire into which we pushed long, dried bamboo stalks. The sealed sections of the stalks exploded as satisfactorily, as loudly, and more safely than firecrackers. We sometimes had real firecrackers, but they were not as much fun as the bamboo poles. After the bonfire and bamboo fireworks, we usually had a screened-porch picnic (to discourage mosquitoes and gnats) with hot dogs and the proper foods to accompany hot dogs, like baked beans and potato salad, always ending with a watermelon that had been chilled in cold water from the well. Of course the flag flew again for the Fourth of July. Sometimes we had our picnic on the banks of the Creek so that we could swim and cool off in the July heat.

I do not recall special celebrations for Labor Day.

For Halloween, we went to the Halloween carnival at the school where my mother was teaching or, when we were older and more responsible, at whatever school we attended. Sometimes we had costumes, but mostly we did not. At the Halloween carnivals, there were booths set up by the various grades to earn money by selling food—brownies, fudge, cakes, pies—which the parents had made. There was usually a house of horrors, too. It was not very scary, but we pretended it was.

For Armistice Day, the flag flew once more. It was still called Armistice Day until 1954, when it became Veterans' Day. The change of name brought home to us all the sad truth that there was no such thing as "the war to end all wars."

For Thanksgiving, we had a "big" dinner. We had chicken cooked until it was very tender, mashed potatoes with gravy, *knoedel* (a boiled, seasoned bread pudding), cranberry sauce, green peas, and pumpkin pie. That was a feast for us, since many meals consisted of beans of some sort, potatoes, and usually not much meat. Such meals were ample and nourishing but not very special.

A Sunday night supper usually consisted of saltine crackers, covered with melted Velveeta cheese, and a pitcher of hot cocoa, but that followed an ample Sunday noon dinner. "Dinner" came in the *middle* of the day, "supper" at *night*.

Christmas was the big holiday of the year. My aunt came to visit, and we knew that she had brought good things with her. We stood a pine from our woods in the parlor on Christmas Eve morning and decorated it with German ornaments that had been in the Pflug family since my mother, aunt, and uncle were children. There were glass balls and beautiful glass birds among the decorations, and there were real wax candles in metal holders that clipped onto the ends of the branches. The waxy, smoky scent of the candles blended perfectly with the fresh pine scent of the tree. We were careful not to leave any candles burning when we left the room.

Quite often, we put green moss around the base of the tree that rested in a stand my father had made using the heavy metal wheel from a car. The moss concealed the wheel and made it look, we pretended, as though the tree were still in the forest.

My mother baked: pecan macaroons; Christmas sugar cookies; *vanille kipfeln*—round, crescent-shaped cookies rolled in confectioner's sugar mixed with the contents of a vanilla bean, if we could find whole, dried vanilla beans—a rarity during the war; finger *kolache*—sugar cookies topped with cherry jam; and a *gugelhupf*—a coffee cake with raisins, maraschino cherries, and pecans. One Christmas, my mother and I made marzipan, but we decided we liked our traditional baked goods better. On Christmas Eve, we exchanged gifts and sang Christmas songs while my mother played the piano. Christmas morning, we emptied our stockings that had hung by the fireplace all night. Christmas dinner was a repetition of the Thanksgiving meal, thus a very special, enjoyable meal for us.

All of the holidays left us with good memories, except for the Christmas when we were sad because Victor was not able to come home. That was in 1941, after the Japanese attack on Pearl Harbor on December 7, when all servicemen were restricted within areas close to their bases. Victor was in the navy, based in Norfolk, and spent his Christmas there. It was the first time in my life that the living members of our immediate family had not all been together for the holiday.

Did you have medical care?

Medical care was mostly homegrown, because our distance from Green Cove Springs and Jacksonville and the expense of medical care precluded rushing to a doctor if anything untoward happened. If a problem developed into something my parents felt they were not able to handle with home care, then, yes, a doctor would be consulted, but that very seldom was the case. My parents became quite good at determining the seriousness of a bump, bruise, illness, cut, or whatever bacterial or viral disease might afflict us, and we all knew that time and rest were the best cures.

Fortunately, this philosophy never backfired on us.

As a result, the only family doctor I knew personally was Dr. Swift, who owned an office in Orange Park. He diagnosed the need for tonsil removal for my brothers and me, recommended injections to keep me from catching colds so easily, and generally was available when we might need him.

Aside from Dr. Swift, I recall only Dr. Rasmussen, my grandmother's friend, creator of the awful Rasol mentioned earlier.

My brothers and I were delivered at Riverside Hospital in Jacksonville—Victor by Dr. Freeman, Gerald by Dr. James D. Pasco, and I by Dr. J. G. Barfield. Our mother rented a room very near Riverside Hospital for the final weeks of her last three pregnancies in order to avoid repeating the tragedy of the stillbirth of her first child, for which she blamed herself for the remainder of her life.

We received the federally required vaccinations for smallpox, typhoid, and diphtheria at the schools we attended and generally remained very healthy in spite of hard times. The traveling school nurses provided vaccinations, kept a watch for serious problems among the school children, and recommended that seriously ill children be taken to doctors.

When my grandmother suffered a stroke in 1939, my mother, grandmother, brothers, and I lived in a rented house directly across the street from the Orange Park School so that my mother could continue teaching and also care for Grandma. My brothers and I helped as much as we could by keeping Grandma company when we were home from school. Further care for Grandma was difficult, because she did not want to be away from her home, but my mother had to continue working to help support us. Earl stayed at the Black Creek property to care for it.

Over the years, Grandma had several caretakers in our home, hired by my mother, and was briefly in at least two different rest homes. She didn't like the caretakers and hated the homes, so when she was bedridden with later strokes, for one semester Gerald and I stayed with her on alternate days to take care of her. This was not a problem because we had plenty of time to keep up with our schoolwork and homework. Then for the last three years of Grandma's life, my mother stopped teaching and stayed home full-time with her, returning to teaching only after my grandmother's death in 1946.

So there it is—my personal account of life in the early twentieth century. I am typing this in 2014, sitting at a fine, new computer in my comfortably climate-controlled home in south Florida, with two indoor bathrooms, both with running water, hot and cold.

The only bamboo on my property is a huge one with widely spaced, giant canes planted by a previous owner. I wonder each Fourth of July what impressive explosions its segments might make in a bonfire, but a bonfire is not permitted here.

In my kitchen, I have wonderful appliances that make cooking, baking, and storing food much easier than in the preelectricity days of my childhood. My dirty dishes are washed by an efficient machine. My laundry needs no wringing out by hand or hanging on a line to dry. My lamps are fitted with fluorescent or LED bulbs. If I need groceries, I drive my air-conditioned car less than one mile on a smoothly paved road to the nearest Publix Market.

Also close by are pharmacies, hardware stores, service stations, department stores, beauty parlors, one very modern hospital, doctors' and dentists' offices, a state college, several universities, theaters, auditoriums, schools, an interstate highway, and whatever else modern life might demand. The ocean is only a mile away, but it lacks the compelling charm of Black Creek, and the freighters and cruise ships passing by hold no magic for me.

Sadly, with the passage of time I have realized that the beautiful yachts carrying the beautiful people on the Creek were among the major contributors to the erosion of the shoreline and pollution of the Creek waters of my early life. There is a lesson there, I think.

If I want to visit my brother on the old home property in North Florida, I can drive the 286.92 miles from my house in South Florida to his house on Black Creek in only a few minutes more than the amount of time it took my grandparents to travel a few miles to Jacksonville by boat from their dock.

I am spoiled.

Would I change it all for the earlier times if I could? Probably not, because I know what has *already* happened, and I know I could neither make the good things better nor prevent the bad things from happening. Now I want to know what will happen *next*, and I intend to stay around as long as I am allowed, to find out. I wish I could be here to read the ensuing chapters of this story, when someone else writes them.

Family image

APPENDICES

APPENDIX 1

Robert Earl Thorp Biography, by Augusta Pflug Thorp 1955

1883—Born in Seneca, Missouri, fifth child of George Washington and Jane Ball Thorp. Two sisters, Fannie and Maggie, and one brother, Wilbur, were living. The oldest, Alonzo, died in childhood of diphtheria.

1885—Moved to Conway Springs, Kansas.

1886—Taught to say "Hurrah!" for Grover Cleveland.

1888—Started school at Conway Springs four-teacher elementary school.

1890—Brother Wilbur accidentally killed when .22 rifle went off. *(See appendix 7.)*

1891—Grew up in father's blacksmith shop and Old Man Fitch's gun shop.

1893—Opening of Cherokee Strip in Oklahoma by horse-race. G. W. Thorp tried unsuccessfully to stake a claim.

1896—Cheering for [William Jennings] Bryan. Slogan was "In eighteen hundred and ninety-six, McKinley went crazy over politics!"

1897—Attended Conway Springs Normal and Business College. Spent summers working on ranches in Colorado, Oklahoma, Texas, and Mexico.

1898—Great celebration for [Commodore] Dewey in Manila.

1901—Joined army. Went to Manila in the Philippines.

1902—Got into an ambush at San Pedro Makadi and was shot in head. Discharged after many weeks in First Reserve Hospital in Manila. Returned to U.S.

1903—Went to sea on sailing ship *Astral* from San Francisco to New York around Cape Horn.

1904—About this time, Earl's father and sister, Maggie, made a trip to Oklahoma where land was offered in the Kickapoo-Kiowa-Caddo lottery in what is now Kiowa County. Again, no luck.

1905—Went on other sailing ships to South America, Mexico, Cuba, Porto (now "Puerto") Rico, and across Atlantic.

1906—Sailed to Australia.

1907—Returned to New York via South Africa, India, etc.

1908—Voted for first time (Taft).

1909—Still going to sea coastwise, with interludes of work ashore.

1910—Earl's father arrived in Florida and bought twenty-five acres of land at Russell across railroad from Russell post office and north.

1911—Returned to Kansas, operating own machine and welding shop at Conway Springs.

1916—Earl came to Florida with his father and mother, driving 1914 Model T Ford. Trip took about fifteen days, (about 1200 miles). Roads under water for many miles in Mississippi. There were only three other cars in Clay County at that time.

1917—Earl's father traded 25 acres at Russell for relinquishment on 80-acre homestead to Bill Baxley. Built house.

1918—Joined Navy. Yachting cruise on Submarine Chaser to Adriatic, Base 25, Corfu, Greece. Later Spaleto, Dalmatia. Shoulder knocked out of place by [head of] sledge hammer flying off handle. [USS *Leonidas*, (1898–1922, later *AD-7*)] *(See appendix 3.)*

1919—Served in the American Relief Administration, Trieste, with Herbert Hoover.

1920—Returned to U.S. and to Florida for Easter. Married June 19. Employed by Murphy Iron Works, Jacksonville.

1921—Mulberry, Florida. Employed by Phosphate Mine Shop.

1923—Victor born, September 25.

1924—Construction work at Penney Farms. Made model of Green Cove spring.

1927—Gerald born, October 24.

1930—Operated shop in Doctor's Inlet—Garage.

1931—Alice Marie born, December 19.

1942—Hawaii, Pearl Harbor Navy Yard. Civil Service. *(See appendix 2.)*

1945—Returned from Pearl Harbor.

1950—Became father-in-law, December 30 (Marion and Gerald).

1951—Became father-in-law, October 13 (Carmen and Victor).

Became grandpa, November 18 David Scharrer Thorp (Gerald and Marion).

1952—"You never had it so good." (?) (Truman).

1953—Became grandpa, January 16 Terry Catherine Thorp (Gerald and Marion).

1954—Became father-in-law, October 23 (Ralph and Alice).

1954—Became grandpa, March 21, Gordon Andrew Thorp (Victor and Carmen).

1955—Became grandpa, June 3, Suzanne Marguerite Thorp (Gerald and Marion).

1957—Became grandpa, Brian George Thorp, December 2, (Victor and Carmen).

1961—Died after surgery, Clay County Hospital, Green Cove Springs, Florida.

Letter Written by Earl, December 26, 1941, Beginning of World War II

Hon. Frank Knox
Secretary of the Navy
Subject: Request for permission to re-enlist

Sir:

I request permission to re-enlist in the U.S. Navy for combat service in a submarine chaser or destroyer, and the closer to Japan the better it would suit me.

I realize that I am over-age and not in first-class physical condition, but I am able and anxious to do my part in the scrap.

I enclose a statement from my last employer to show that I am able to climb around the frame of a building and do a day's work, which, I think, would indicate that I can still get around aboard ship. *(Alice: Statement lost.)*

I started to sea in the days of wooden ships and iron men. I was seaman, boatswain, second mate, and first mate aboard sail ships. On steamers I was seaman, quartermaster and second mate.

I am fifty-eight years old, have a hernia which is so well held in place by an appliance that it has never bothered me in eighteen years. I have ten teeth in my lower jaw and a full set of upper teeth, practically new, which fit well.

As a boy I started to learn the trade of machinist and tool maker in a gunsmith shop. I still make my own taps and reamers, and can make an internal combustion motor behave.

I was M.M. 2C aboard *U.S.S.C 324* and Bsmith 1C on board *U.S.S. Leonidas* and ex-Austrian ship *Zrinyi* during and after World War I.

With my previous sea experience I would not need any training to go aboard a sub-chaser and GET submarines. I am ready to go on twenty-four hours' notice. Would not say that I must have any special rate or station. Want to be where I can do the most good. If nothing better, would accept a canoe, take my own knife, and emulate my ancestors by garnering some scalps. My wife can get along without my help and is willing to try it.

Respectfully, R.E. Thorp

Letters Related to Earl's Request for Disability

CHARACTER REFERENCES BY SHIPMATES

4537 Commonwealth Ave
Detroit, Michigan
March 8, 1934

To Whom It May Concern

Dear Sir

Recently I received a letter from R.E. THORP, residing at Russell Florida, requesting that I furnish him an affidavit concerning an injury received by him while he was employed as a blacksmith on the *U.S. Leonidas.*

R.E. Thorp and I were shipmates on the *S.C. 324* and later on the *H.M.S. Zrinyi* in the U.S. service. It was while he was on the first mentioned ship that he received and answered a request from the *U.S.S. Leonidas* for a blacksmith and was transferred aboard her in that capacity.

The injury to which he lays his present disability happened one afternoon while he was engaged with the assistance of another man in cutting a steel plate by hand, which was one of his duties as blacksmith. Thorp was holding the cutting hammer and his partner was swinging the sledge hammer. His partner was using a full arm swing when the head of his heavy hammer came off and struck Thorp high on the right part of his chest and shoulder. The force of the blow knocked Thorp over, and when he recovered, outside of being bruised, it did not show at the time any other injury.

My knowledge of this injury and the manner and time in which it was received comes from the fact that I, on official business for the vessel on which I happened to be stationed at the time, came aboard the *Leonidas* a few minutes after the accident and having a few minutes to spare looked for Thorp and found him. I received the story of the accident from him and the men present at the time it happened.

A short time later Thorp and I were shipmates on the *H.M.S. Zrinyi* and I often asked him how his shoulder and chest felt. He always had the same answer to the effect that it felt all right. This answer is typical from a man like Thorp, he never wanted to give in or complain, although I sensed at the time that he was in pain and suffering. In my knowledge of Thorp as a shipmate and personal friend he was one of the best. He worked hard and never complained no matter what the circumstances were.

I am glad that I am in a position to write this letter since I am sure Thorp will appreciate any help that I am able to give him.

Stanley R. Guernsey
Federal Post No. 373, American Legion

AFFIDAVIT

STATE OF NEW YORK
COUNTY OF NEW YORK

John J. Shively, being duly sworn, deposes and says:

That he served in the Sub-Chaser fleet in the Eastern Mediterranean aboard the *U.S.S.C. 255*, later on the *U.S.S. Leonidas*, and finally on the *S.M.S. Zrinyi*.

That his recollection of an injury sustained by R.E. Thorp while the latter was working as blacksmith aboard the *U.S.S. Leonidas* is as follows:

On the day of the accident a shipmate informed the deponent that Thorp had been struck by the head of a sledge and was in the sick bay or hospital. Later, an eye witness described the accident, stating to the deponent that Thorp's helper was using a heavy sledge with a full arm swing against a tool which Thorp was holding, when the head of the sledge flew off, striking Thorp high on the right chest and shoulder and knocking him down. Deponent recollects that it was remarked Thorp must be [made] of iron, and that such a blow either on the head or over the heart would have killed him instantly.

Later deponent served as first assistant engineering officer on the *S.M.S. Zrinyi*, on which vessel Thorp was also stationed. In observing Thorp's work, deponent noted several times that he was having difficulty with his right arm and shoulder, and inquired about his injury? Thorp stoically refused to complain, taking the attitude that hard knocks were part of the game, and that as the work must be done it was up to him to do it.

From his acquaintances with and observation of Thorp, deponent found him to be a man of excellent character and a hard worker with a very high sense of duty. In view of his knowledge of Thorp's character, together with the above stated recollections concerning the latter's injury, deponent is firmly convinced that Thorp's present disability is the direct result of that injury.

(Signed) John J. Shively State of New York

On the 8ᵗʰ day of August, 1934, personally appeared before me John J. Shively, to me personally known and known to me to be the individual described in and who executed the foregoing instrument, and acknowledged that he executed the same.

(Signed) Edna B. Isler, Notary Public

APPENDIX 4

Curriculum Vitae
Marguerite L. Pflug

(By Her Own Hand)

Place of Birth: Austria

Father: Max O. Pflug Mother: Marie Fischer

Family came to America in 1898

Naturalized citizen in 1905

Early education in Austria, New Jersey, Germany, Switzerland

Ph.B. John B. Stetson University 1914

M.A. Columbia University 1932

Advanced graduate work at Columbia, University of Geneva, University of Berlin

Teacher of French & German, Virginia Intermont College, Bristol, Va., 1914–1921

Academic Dean & Professor of French & German, (same college), 1921–1957

Associate Professor of French & German, King College, Bristol, Tennessee, 1957–1970

Associate Professor Emerita of Modern Foreign Languages (same college) 1970–1972

Instructor in German at Columbia University while on leave of absence, 1929–1930

Director of V.I. Ranch Camp, Bristol, Tennessee-Virginia, summers of 1936–1941

Member and local examiner of Red Cross Life Saving Corps, 1921–1941

Conductor of College tours to Europe, 1925–1935

Delta Delta Delta

Women in Administration, 1950–1957

Delta Kappa Gamma

Woman's History Club, President 1955–1957 & other offices

Circle Chairman, First Presbyterian Church, 1956

Bristol Branch of the Tennessee Ornithological Society, President 1951–1952 & others

A. A.U.W.

Board of Directors of Bristol, Y.W.C.A.

Sponsor of Phi Theta Kappa at Virginia Intermont College from granting of Charter to 1957

American Association of Teachers of French

American Association of Teachers of German

Modern Language Association of America

South Atlantic Modern Language Association

South Atlantic Association of Teachers of German, Charter Member

Ancestors were preachers and professors in Leipzig and Wittenberg, Germany

Father was in exporting business, Germany

Listed in Personalities Of The South, 1969

Church affiliation: Presbyterian

Favorite hymn: Holy, Holy, Holy, Lord God Almighty

Favorite Scripture Passage: *Twenty-Third Psalm*

Hobbies and special interests: Wild flowers, birds, languages, travel, reading, music, Renaissance art, etc., World fellowship

Letters in Academic Tug-of-War, 1916

March 23, 1916

Miss Marguerite Pflug,
Intermont College,
Bristol, VA.

My dear Miss Pflug:

On account of ill health, Miss Whiting does not wish to return next year. I write to offer you a position in Modern Languages; three classes in French and three in German. Two of these classes will be very small, numbering only a few who will want a third year. They will all be in the Academy. If there should be only four Modern Language classes, I should want you to teach one subject in some other line and hold down one study hall period. You know the usual outside duties of chaperones here. I should want your sympathetic co-operation. The compensation would be $500.00 and home, the home to include table board, room, light and heat.

That is the offer. In addition I want you to come. Please give me your earliest possible answer.

Very sincerely yours,

[Dr. Lincoln Hulley]
President [Stetson]

March 27, 1916

Dr. Lincoln Hulley
De Land, Fla.

Dear Dr. Hulley:

Miss Pflug showed me your letter. I feel sure that you were not aware that she has already signed her contract with us for session 1916-17. As we shall have several other changes in our faculty, it would embarrass us only the more to have to make a change in our French and German Department. Miss Pflug, of course, feels complimented that she should be asked to return to her alma mater, but as yet she has not asked us to release her. Of course from our standpoint, we feel that she ought to remain.

Sincerely yours,

[H.G. Noffsinger,]
President
[Virginia Intermont College]

March 30, 1916

President H.G. Noffsinger,
Virginia Intermont College,
Bristol, VA

Dear Mr. President:

Your kind letter of March 27 is before me. I was not aware, as you correctly premised, that you had offered a contract to Miss Pflug for next year. We have looked forward here to Miss Pflug's return. She has not known this, and we rarely have vacancies. If you were not to grant her release now, it would prevent her coming at all. Of course a contract must be kept, and if you will not release her, neither she nor I will question your right. If you should see fit to release her, I am sure I can recommend a good teacher to take her place. She would not be available for us, because she graduates this year.

Very kindly yours,

[Dr. Lincoln Hulley]
President. [Stetson]

Virginia Intermont College
Bristol, Virginia

April 2, 1916

My dear Dr. Hulley,

Although willing to release me from my contract if I should insist upon it, Mr. Noffsinger has made me feel that, in so doing, I should place the school at a great disadvantage. I have therefore decided to stay another year.

I want to thank you again for your very kind offer.

Very sincerely yours,

Marguerite Pflug

Oscar Pflug's Adventure, Pre-World War I, as Reported in the New York Times

GERARD HAS GERMAN IN PARTY ARRESTED

Denounces Oscar Pflug As a Suspect and French Authorities Hold Him.

Served On Embassy Staff

Hired in Envoy's Absence—Confused When Questioned At Border—Gerard Reaches Paris.

Special Cable to THE NEW YORK TIMES

PARIS, Feb. 15 [1917]—James W. Gerard, recently the American Ambassador to Germany, arrived from Berne this morning with his party.

The crossing of the French border was marked by an interesting episode at Pontarlier at about 1 o'clock in the morning. The former envoy personally denounced a man who had traveled with his party from Berlin, as a suspect, with the immediate result that the French authorities immediately detained the man for further examination, the results of which are unknown to those of us who came on to Paris.

The person who aroused Mr. Gerard's suspicion was Oscar Pflug, a young man who had been employed in a minor capacity in the American Embassy at Berlin for several months. He entered the Embassy service during Mr. Gerard's absence last Summer. When employed, he was subjected to a careful examination. Several of the members of the Embassy force questioned him, and his case was carefully considered. He is of American Birth, but of German descent, and had correct papers. The circumstances generally seemed all right and satisfactory.

Mr. Gerard personally had very little to do with Pflug and saw little of him; in fact, hardly knew the man. When the time came to arrange for the departure from Berlin, Pflug came along as one of the Embassy staff. Mr. Gerard was not personally cognizant of the details of the arrangement for departure and was not aware that several persons, who did obtain the advantage of coming on his train, were minimally members of his party.

Pflug, however, made himself conspicuous during the trip from Berlin to Zurich, being constantly associated with the German officer in charge of the train. Pflug was so much in evidence that several of those making the trip got the impression that he was somehow officially concerned in handling the train.

He was less conspicuous about Berne, but when Mr. Gerard's party left last night, Pflug had a place on the train.

The French officials at Berne had been most courteous to all bona-fide members of the Ambassadorial party, but there had been such pressure from outsiders to create the impression of being attached to Gerard's coatskirts that the examination at Pontarlier was considerably dragged out.

All those entitled to diplomatic courtesy through genuine connection with Mr. Gerard were passed speedily by the French authorities. Then came a crowd of additional Americans, near-Americans, naturalized Americans, and once-naturalized Americans who had lost their legal right to claim American citizenship.

Something about Pflug attracted the attention of the French authorities. He had got his hand luggage through in the first rush and had placed himself on Mr. Gerard's special train. Mr. Gerard had given no authority for that, and when it came to his notice he promptly ordered Pflug off the train. That seemed to arouse his interest in Pflug and he began to question the man. Pflug became confused and presently was caught in contradictions and statements which were known to be untrue.

Suddenly Gerard ended the matter by turning to the French authorities, exclaiming: "This man is a suspect."

That ended Pflug's chances of getting on that train and probably on any other for some time.

Mr. Gerard interested himself, then, to see that all those rightfully entitled to get through were promptly passed.

The Ambassador's party had a special train. Most of the other Americans who left Berlin on Mr. Gerard's train came from Pontarlier on the regular train, which ran close behind Mr. Gerard's special, all arriving in Paris practically together.

From the beginning of the difficulties in Berlin Mr. Gerard had been subjected to great pressure to lend the cover of his diplomatic status to all sorts of persons, who had no claim to such consideration. Getting distressed Americans out of Germany was one thing. There they might be compelled to undergo the hardships of a prison camp. But in Switzerland they were free from that menace. Getting them from Switzerland into France was an entirely different matter.

The French authorities held at Pontarlier also an American doctor, who had been working a few weeks in German hospitals. He was the son of German parents. His case seemed to have nothing suspicious about it, except his descent, and he probably will be along soon.

ACQUAINTANCE HERE TELLS OF YOUTH DETAINED AT GERARD'S INSTANCE

NEW YORK TIMES

February 18, 1917: Harry R. Tompkins of the Universal Safety Mattress Company, 31 Nassau Street, New York City writes to THE TIMES concerning Oscar Pflug, the youth detained by the French authorities at Pontparlier when Mr. Gerard, on whose train he came from Germany as a former member of the Embassy Staff, declared him a suspect. Mr. Tompkins says he has been acquainted with Pflug nine of his twenty-five years of life, and adds:

"I know him as a loyal American citizen and a very honorable young man."

Mr. Tompkins goes on:

"Oscar M. Pflug attended either the Montclair Military Academy or the Montclair High School for several Years and resided on High Street, Newark, N.J. with his parents. He later moved to Bloomfield and, finally, when his parents moved to Rideout, Clay County, Fla., resided at the Standish Arms, Brooklyn. Upon completing his education, he accepted a position with the Astor Trust Company, Fifth Avenue, and later went into business with his father under the name of the New Netherland Trading Company, Exchange Place, New York. In January, 1913, he sailed for England to become the agent in Germany for the Stuart Carburetor Company of London. His place of business was in Hanover, and he was engaged in this work until war was declared, which cut off his connections with England, thus ruining his business.

"During the five years that the writer associated with him, can assure you that his intimate friends were almost exclusively American boys, whose parents and ancestors for generations had been born in this country. Although his parents were born on the other side and he had many relatives there, he always considered himself an American.

As an illustration of his American spirit, an incident that he related to me as occurring while on a trip to Germany causes me to consider it worthwhile repeating now. He was in a Post Office building and was requested by a policeman to remove his hat, which he refused to do, asking why he should. He was then informed that this was necessary in honor of the Kaiser and he said he was an American and did not feel like extending any honors in that direction. He was consequently arrested and taken to a police station, where an appeal to friends was made, and he was released.

"The writer has heard from him by postal [card] and letter all during the last four years, and received the last letter about a month ago, in which he stated that he had secured passage on a Scandinavian steamship, so that he would have reached home in time for Christmas, but that a chance to rearrange some of his business affairs caused him to cancel the reservation and postpone his return indefinitely.

"In concluding, the writer realizes he can furnish no actual proofs of Oscar M. Pflug's actions while employed by the American Embassy, but he feels absolutely certain of the loyalty of this man to his country."

Harry R. Tompkins

MAX PFLUG PLEADS FOR SON'S RELEASE

SPECIAL TO THE NEW YORK TIMES

Washington, D.C., Feb. 21, [1917] Appeal was made today by Max Pflug of Rideout, Fla., to the State Department to use its good offices to obtain the release of his son, Oscar Pflug, who was turned over to the French authorities by Ambassador Gerard when the latter reached French territory. Young Pflug was employed in the embassy at Berlin. His conduct while the Ambassador's party was leaving Germany, especially his familiarity with German officers, was alleged to have aroused the suspicions of Mr. Gerard.

OSCAR PFLUG RELEASED

Embassy Employe Was Taken from Gerard's Party in France

THE NEW YORK TIMES

Paris, March 6, [1917]—The French Government today ordered the release of Oscar Pflug, a former employe of the American Embassy in Berlin. The release was made on representations by the American Ambassador.

Oscar Pflug was one of several persons detained by the French authorities when Ambassador Gerard's party entered France. Pflug's replies to questions put to him were said to have been unsatisfactory, and he was held pending further investigation. Although Pflug had been employed at the embassy in Berlin his name did not appear in the public records of American diplomatic and consular employes, he having been engaged provisionally at Berlin during the press of business.

Max Pflug, father of the man, who lives in Rideout, Florida, recently appealed to the State Department to use its good offices in obtaining the release of Pflug.

A True Account of Wilber's Death

A Tragic Account, Typed Without Corrections, as Handwritten by M.M. Orr [Earl's Sister]

It was Wednesday, June 17, 1891. We had just eaten our first meal in the new dining room and Mamma and Fanny were washing the kitchen furniture. I was clearing away the dinner dishes, Papa was putting a pane in one of the dining-room windows, Mr. McMain was doing some carpenter work, and Mamma had sent Wilber and Earl upon the old kitchen to throw some bricks and lime off. (We had had the chimney taken off and there was some lime and pieces of brick up there yet and as it was windy, the lime would blow down and into our eyes.) To get upon the roof the boys had to go through the upstairs window. When they had thrown all of the bricks off, Earl came down, but Wilber stayed up there a little longer to hand a bucket of lime down to Mamma. When he got ready to come down he crawled through the upstairs window and called some of us to come put the window down. We told him to put it down but he said he couldn't, so Mamma said "Maggie go and put it down, he can't." I went and I have wished—I can't tell how often that I had never went. However I <u>did</u> go and when I started up the stairway, I closed the door behind me. Wilber was sitting at the head of the stairs. I went on up and as I started to put the window down, he rose and closed it himself, saying, as he did so, something to the effect that he could put it down and that he didn't need my help. He had something of mockery in his tone, as if he had called me up there only for fun. He sat down again and as I had left my beads upstairs, I started on past him to get them. As I did so, he picked up the gun which was lying beside him and pointing it at me, said "And so here is the gun." I said, "Yes here is the gun," and telling him to let me see it a minute. I took it and resumed, "and here is the trigger." I pulled the trigger but, as the hammer was not cocked, it did not go off. I cocked the hammer and holding the gun at an angle of about 45 degrees, told him to shut his eyes. He did so, but did not shut them tight enough to not see me. So I said, "Now Wilber, honest, shut yours eyes tight. I placed the nozzle of the gun right at his left nostril and pulled the trigger. (Not knowing or even dreaming that the gun was loaded.)

When the gun went off, his eyes rolled back and I realized that I had shot my own brother. I was so surprised at the gun going off that I sat still and looked at Wilber for as much as 10 seconds any way. I hurriedly picked him up and started down-stairs with him calling all the time for Mamma but as I could not make myself heard, I dropped him, about half way down the steps and went on calling for Mamma. I met her in the back door and told her what I had done and she rushed on telling me to call Papa. I went on to the dining room door and told Fannie and she and I went back into the other house where we met Mamma with Wilber in her arms. (Papa had heard us and came in and went for the doctor but I didn't know that he had went for the doctor.) I ran to Mamma and caught W. by the head and rubbed my hand over his face calling to him to see if I could not get an ans. To prove that he was still alive.

Mamma told me to tell Mr. McMain to run for the doctor. I did so and then ran for the Dr. myself. As I passed Mr. Gosney's, I ran in to see if they had seen papa go by but as they hadn't I went on after telling them about it. Bareheaded and bloody, I ran into the gate at the house of Dr. Farris and asked Mrs. F. if the Dr. was there, but she said she thought that he was down at the office. As I started to the office, I saw Papa pass and he asked me if he [Wilber] was dead. I told him I didn't know, and went on. I went down and found the Dr. and told him I wished he would hurry. I started back and found Mrs. Farris and Mrs. Ike Chenoweth back of the furniture store.

I stayed with them a little while, and then went over to Farris's and washed my hands and face. I then came up home and the Dr. was here, also several of the neighbors. Papa was crying in the old Kitchen, Mamma was out in the new kitchen crying and Fanny and Earl was crying and of course, I was crying too. Wilber groaned in such way as to run me nearly wild. I couldn't bear to hear him.

So Earl and I went down to Mr. Gosney's for a little while. When we came back, Papa was hunting for me. He wanted me to show him how Wilber and I were sitting etc., so that they could tell whether the bullet had come out or lodged in his head. (I don't know yet whether it came out or not.) Mamma and I went over to Goble's where I stayed the rest of Wilber's life.

Mr. Goble's folks were very kind to me as indeed, was everybody. My girl friends (Lonie Hall, Emma Gwin, and May Graham) were very kind to me too, staying out of school to be with me and cheer me. Everybody was kinder to me than I ever deserved. I the next thing to a murderess—thank them for all their kindness.

I understand that Papa blamed himself. But it was all my own fault. The way the gun happened to be loaded is –

The men down town were having a kind of shooting match. They all wanted to try Papa's new gun and so they were shooting at a target. Papa put a load in it and aimed to shoot it off at a dog, I believe, but forgot to unload the gun or shoot the dog either.

He had never left the gun loaded before.

Wilber died on Thursday night, June 18, 1891, and was buried Friday, June 19, 1891 at about 5 o'clock.

Friends, you have read my story if you want to condemn me I am here—do as you like with me.

Maggie Thorp

Program for Graduation at Orange Park School, April 23, 1925

Song: "Schooldays"—School

"The Schoolbell"—Jack Beyers

"Flags of Many Lands"—4th and 5th grades

"Johnny's History Lesson"—Harold Clay

"My Auto 'tis of Thee"—Trio: Pauljames Weigand, Aleck Gilmore, Henry Howard

"V-a-c-a-t-i-o-n"—Primary grades

Dumbell Drill—Evangeline Strom, Minnie Harvey, Rosamond Weigand, Gladys Merrian

"A Lesson in Elocution"—6th, 7th, 8th grade boys

Song—"Florida"—School

Essay—"History of Orange Park"—Evangeline Strom

Essay—"History of Orange Park"—Pauljames Weigand

Debate: Resolved that Hunting is better Sport than Fishing.

Affirmative Negative

Pauljames Evangeline

Harry Henry

Earl J.F.

Aleck George

Ballot [Presumably this was to decide the winning side of the debate.]

Prophecy—George Morrison

Presentation of Diplomas

Roses—Gladys Morrison

Valedictory—Evangeline Strom

"God be With You"—School and audience

School Attended by Augusta and Marguerite

MISS TOWNSEND'S SCHOOL FOR GIRLS

54 PARK PLACE, NEWARK, NEW JERSEY

Miss Townsend's School was established in 1891 as a home and day school. There are three departments: Lower Intermediate, Upper Intermediate, and Academic. The certificate of the School admits to the leading colleges and is accepted by the University of the State of New York. A Latin and an English course are available for students who do not intend to enter college.

The School is located in Military Park and is in easy walking distance of the important railway depots. The building is large, the rooms well furnished and ventilated. The teachers represent the leading colleges. French and German are taught by native teachers. A limited number of boarding pupils are received and given advantages of a refined and attractive home life.

Personal attention is given to health, manners, and development of character. For circular, address

MISS ANNA P. TOWNSEND, Principal

Fin.